Praise for Lisa Scottoline and Francesca Serritella

"Readers can count on an ab-toning laugh session, a silly giggle, a sympathetic sigh, and a lump in the throat as life's moments are rehashed through the keen eyes and wits of this lovable mother-daughter duo."
—*Booklist* on *Meet Me at Emotional Baggage Claim*

"Essays that are fun to read, share, and ponder."
—*Publishers Weekly* on *Meet Me at Emotional Baggage Claim*

"Despite all the 'emotional baggage' they carry (and fearlessly claim), however, their faith in and commitment to each other remains unshaken because, writes Scottoline, 'that's love' . . . Erma Bombeck for mothers and daughters, with a zesty Italian twist."
—*Kirkus Reviews* on *Meet Me at Emotional Baggage Claim*

"Feels like one big gabfest with your best girlfriends, whatever their age."
—*Booklist* on *Best Friends, Occasional Enemies*

"[A] witty and sweet return to the ins and outs of life in the sometimes kooky, always smart and funny, family."
—*Publishers Weekly* on *Best Friends, Occasional Enemies*

"A clever compilation from two generations of women reflecting on family, love, dessert, and everything in between."
—*Booklist* on *My Nest Isn't Empty, It Just Has More Closet Space*

"Rueful, uplifting, sweet, kooky—and always amusing."
—*Publishers Weekly* on *My Nest Isn't Empty,*
It Just Has More Closet Space

"Delightfully witty."   —*AudioFile* on *My Nest Isn't Empty,*
It Just Has More Closet Space

"One of the best double acts in the business."
—*Connecticut Post* on *My Nest Isn't Empty,*
It Just Has More Closet Space

"Shrewd, tart, sensitive, and hard to resist."
—*Kirkus Reviews* on
Why My Third Husband Will Be a Dog

"The perfect present for moms, grandmas, and aunts."
—*Cosmopolitan* on
Why My Third Husband Will Be a Dog

"Scottoline savors every last bit of her life, and so will you."
—*People* on *Why My Third Husband Will Be a Dog*

Meet Me at Emotional Baggage Claim

Lisa Scottoline

AND

Francesca Serritella

ST. MARTIN'S GRIFFIN ✖ NEW YORK

www.stmartins.com

All photographs courtesy of the authors.

The Library of Congress has cataloged the hardcover edition as follows:

Scottoline, Lisa.
    Meet me at emotional baggage claim / Lisa Scottoline and Francesca Serritella. — 1st ed.
        p. cm.
    ISBN 978-0-312-64008-8 (hardcover)
    ISBN 978-1-250-02507-4 (e-book)
    1. Mothers and daughters—Humor.   2. Women—Humor.   3. Scottoline, Lisa.   4. Serritella, Francesca Scottoline.   I. Serritella, Francesca Scottoline. II. Title.
    PN6231.M68S375 2012
    818'.5402—dc23

                                                        2012034515

ISBN 978-1-250-02508-1 (trade paperback)

St. Martin's Griffin books may be purchased for educational, business, or promotional use. For information on bulk purchases, please contact Macmillan Corporate and Premium Sales Department at 1-800-221-7945, extension 5442, or write specialmarkets@macmillan.com.

First St. Martin's Griffin Edition: May 2014

D   10   9   8   7   6   5   4   3   2

To our readers everywhere, with love and thanks

Contents

....

Meet Me at Emotional Baggage Claim

Meet Me at Emotional Baggage Claim

By Lisa

I was just talking with a friend of mine, who says she has to nag her kids every time they leave for a trip. She nags them to pack their bags, to get ready on time, and to not forget their sneakers. She feels bad for nagging them, and all of it takes me back to when Daughter Francesca was ten years old and we had one of the best fights of our life.

And yes, you can have a good fight with your daughter.

If you've read me before, you know that I think fighting is healthy and normal, and a good fight is when you learn something from your kid. Not when you win.

If you win, ten years later, your daughter will turn up pregnant.

Don't try to win. Try to learn.

But I'm getting ahead of myself.

I'll never forget the day of our fight, because it's when I started traveling light.

Now I have it all figured out, especially with respect to nagging. We either do what our mothers did, or we do the exact opposite.

And hopefully, this is a conscious choice, since in due time, if we have any self-awareness at all, we catch on and live the examined life. We figure out our own way to parent, and even to live. We don't have to become our mothers unless we want to.

We have free will, and better shoes.

Most of the time, I want to become Mother Mary. I parent the same way Mother Mary did, in many ways, mainly in loving my kid more than words can say and saying so, complete with hugging, kissing, praising, and celebrating in general.

Mother Mary thinks it's cute when I fart, and that's what we call unconditional love.

Love is such a positive emotion, and kids need to hear it all the time, even grown-up kids. It makes everybody happier, like a hearty plate of spaghetti.

I'm Italian, remember?

But one thing that Mother Mary did not do is nag.

And there's a reason for that.

Let me remind you that Mother Mary grew up as the youngest of nineteen children. This is not a joke. Well, at least, I'm not kidding.

The Flying Scottolines were excellent Catholics, way back when.

Her mother, my grandmother, was married twice because her first husband died, probably from the exertion.

Even Italians have limits.

Anyway, I grew up with Mother Mary telling me stories from her childhood, all of which rival *Angela's Ashes* for their cheeriness. There were siblings who died in infancy. The family was so poor they ate her pet rabbit. There was no money to send anybody to college, and though my mother did well in school, her mother wanted her to drop out and get a job.

Nobody puts Mother Mary in a corner.

She defied her mother, worked while she went to high school, and graduated at the top of her class.

God bless her.

But even her funnier stories from her childhood make it sound like she was raised by wolves. Half the time, her parents didn't know she was around. Once she got pneumonia, and nobody noticed. No one helped her with her homework, got her to a dentist or doctor, or made sure that she had books or clothes, much less that she was dressed and ready for anything on time. In fact, she walked half the city to go to her high school, through some very rough neighborhoods, all by herself.

Needless to say, nobody nagged Mother Mary.

So when she raised me, she didn't know she was supposed to nag me. She didn't get the memo.

She made a decision to be more loving than her mother, and love came naturally to her. But although she loved us, and was there when she needed us, she just wasn't in our business. She always worked as a secretary, and we let ourselves in after school and were generally responsible for ourselves.

Not that I'm complaining. Brother Frank and I had a great childhood. We grew up happy, healthy, and pretty much in charge of our own fates. And when we got burned, we felt the consequences.

So we never did it again.

For example, Brother Frank started to ditch English classes in high school, and my parents didn't catch on until a notice came home saying he wouldn't be able to graduate.

Opera ensued.

My parents went hysterically to the school, which agreed to let him graduate if he went to summer school to make up the classes, but also required him to walk at the end of the processional line at graduation.

This was worse than it sounds.

The processional line was in order of height, and the guy at the end of the line was so tall he went on to play for the NBA.

Brother Frank was five feet, six inches.

At graduation, he looked like a sheepish caboose, or a punctuation mark at the end of capital letters, LIKE THIS.

And everybody laughed, eventually even Frank.

Fast forward to when I become a mother, with a daughter, and in the meantime, the world has changed. Walking at the end of the procession isn't the worst that can happen anymore. There's meth addiction, psycho killers, and reality television.

So you know where this is going.

I started nagging.

When Francesca was little, I nagged her to do her homework, take a bath, clean her room, and wear a heavier coat, and she always told me to stop nagging. Then one day, I remember the morning, she was in fifth grade, and I was rushing her out the door, nagging that we'd be late to school, and she simply burst into tears.

She said, "Mom, you're ignoring me. I'm asking you not to nag me, and you're ignoring what I say."

And I looked at my child, whom I had made cry, her round blue eyes brimming with tears. And finally, I heard her. I realized she was right. She has never been late for anything. She was even born on her due date.

I was nagging her because I needed to nag her, not because she needed to be nagged.

And that's why they call it emotional baggage.

I'm learning to check it, in all senses of the word.

Because I still carry it around, whether it's the way I parent or the way I deal with my daughter, my friends, men, the people I work with, and even my dogs.

Dogs don't have emotional baggage.

And if they did, they'd forget it at the airport.

They know they don't need it.

So I look for when it gets in the way of my relationships, especially mine to Francesca, as she grows older. We are best friends, but we're still smoothing out the wrinkles between us. It's a lifelong process, because we both keep growing, and those wrinkles have made for some of the best, worst, saddest, and funniest moments of my life.

This is a book that chronicles those moments. It's about our lives, my daughter's and mine, living both together and apart, as we both grow older. Precious few books are devoted to a mother's relationship with her adult child, which is crazy, because these bonds become more important, not less, as time goes on.

Family is forever.

So read on.

I bet that these stories will resonate with you, because you've had moments like these, too. The only difference between us is that Francesca and I wrote them down.

And, as you may have guessed, I haven't stopped nagging, not completely, especially not since she moved to New York, where the meth addicts and psycho killers form a processional of their own.

Just kidding.

Though you'll read in the following pages about Francesca's adventures in the big city, complete with her own personal flasher.

The truth is, sometimes nagging is required, and sometimes it isn't, and the most anybody can ask of a mother is that we pause, examine what we're doing and why, then nag if it's in order. Then it's a conscious choice, and we reserve the right to nag.

Because we've lived longer, and we know more. Even if you're an adult child, we're still more adult.

And you have to listen to us. Not because we're your mothers, but because we listen to you.

And that's love.

Forever.

Shakespeare Was No Dummy

· · · · · · · · · · · · · · · · ·

By Lisa

Shakespeare asked, What's in a name? And The Flying Scottolines answered:

Everything.

Last year, Mother Mary was revealed to be Mother Maria, after using the wrong name for eighty-six years. She was unmasked by TSA and the Florida DMV, so now you can rest easy. They've dealt with Mother Mary, and all that's left is Al Qaeda.

By the way, she used to call them Sal Qaeda, but I told her they weren't Italian.

And her name isn't the only problem, historically. My father was named Frank, and so was my brother, which led to confusion around the house. So my father became Big Frank and my brother became Little Frank, and sometimes even Little Frankie.

My brother thinks that's why he's gay, and I believe him.

He was stuck with Little Frankie until he wasn't so Little anymore, when he became Frankie and even opened a bar named Frankie & Johnnie's.

There's a hint for you, new parents. If you're trying to choose a name for your baby, imagine that name on a bar.

If it works for a bar, don't use it for your child.

We come finally to our present problem, which is Daughter Francesca. Her full name is Francesca Scottoline Serritella, which sounds like a federal indictment.

Mafia aside, the other problem is that it's too long for a book cover, even if you just go with Francesca Serritella. Here's another naming hint for new moms and dads. Instead of imagining your child's name on a bar sign, imagine it on a book cover.

Don't underestimate your kid.

Despite your best efforts, they may actually accomplish something.

And also, give them a name they can pronounce. Of course, when Francesca was a baby, she couldn't say Francesca. Many adults can't even say Francesca, including me, after a margarita.

I confess that I didn't think of that when I chose her name. She was named after my father and brother, as well as my best friend Franca, who was named after her own father, Frank.

It's a great name, okay?

So when Francesca was little, she pronounced Francesca as Kiki, and that stuck. Kiki has been her nickname for as long as I can remember, and everybody she knew growing up in grade school and high school called her Kiki.

So far, so good.

But starting college, she decided she wanted to start using her real name, and she introduced herself as Francesca. All her college friends called her Francesca, and in time, that led to confusion, because whether you called her Kiki or Francesca depended on when in her life you had met her, or if you'd actually given birth to her. We'll leave aside for the moment that Mother Mary calls her Cookie, which sounds a lot like Kooky, and we both know who's kooky.

Sal Qaeda.

Francesca doesn't mind if I call her Kiki, but I've noticed it's been a problem, for example, at the doctor's office, which has trouble finding her file because I refer to her as Kiki, but they have her filed under Francesca. And it wasn't so great the other day, when the confusion screwed up a prescription. Plus I've noticed the disconnect myself, when I talk to people and refer to her as Kiki, and then they meet Francesca and find her very nice, but they want to meet my daughter, Kiki.

Also, Kiki works for a bar sign.

Enough said.

Yet, still I persisted with Kiki. Until the other day, when I asked myself why.

Why did I cling to it, creating confusion? She had a preference, which she'd made clear, so why wasn't I honoring it?

Of course, you knew the answer before I did.

What's in a name?

Shakespeare asked that question, but he wasn't a mother.

To me, Francesca was still my baby. But I've decided that has to end.

Because I want my baby to get the right prescription.

And also, for a better reason. Her growing up, through school and college, is the process of forging her own identity. She has the right to define herself, and it begins with her name. She doesn't need to be reminded, every time we speak, that in my eyes, she's just a baby.

Because she's not, anymore.

She's a smart and lovely young woman, with a name that doesn't fit on anything.

And I learned an important lesson.

It's not only new parents who have to choose a name.

Welcome, Francesca.

I love you, already.

I Love You, Man

· · · · · · · · · · · · · · · · ·

By Francesca

My mom and I are total bros.

I realized this when we were at an opening weekend showing of *Mission Impossible 4: Ghost Protocol* in IMAX. We had arrived early to snag prime center seats, and I watched the rest of the audience file in—it was all men. Packs of them, of all ages. Men with their friends, men with their sons, a handful of men with obliging girlfriends. It was as if you needed a Y chromosome to go with your ticket. We were the only women unaccompanied by a penis.

Did this make us uncomfortable?

No way.

Our only regret was not getting the pretzel bites.

You may be thinking that one action movie does not a dude-bro make. I confess that we write a column called "Chick Wit," but you can't judge a book by its pink jacket cover. In our separate lives, we are girls' girls, but when we get together, that all goes out the window.

Allow me to establish our bro cred:

Mission Impossible is only one of our action-movie-franchise loves. My mom sees every action-, superhero-, and testosterone-fueled movie that comes out, but *The Transporter* series is her favorite. If you don't know, these movies feature Jason Stratham shooting up bad guys while driving at about a million miles an hour.

My mom drives 50 mph in a 60 mph zone.

I fancy myself a highbrow bro, so my choice would be the Bourne series. But no matter, we're easy to please. Give us some car chases, explosions, and violence, but skip the gratuitous female nudity. We're like frat guys who are attracted to men.

So we're like frat guys.

Our taste in comedies is equally infused with bro'mones. If a movie is aimed at fourteen-year-old boys, we'll probably dig it. We own copies of such classics as *Dude Where's My Car?, Role Models,* and *Superbad.*

We loved *Deuce Bigalow: Male Gigolo* and hated *Love Actually.*

I'm surprised we don't pee standing up.

I think these movies fried our brain, because we actually suggested *Did You Just Fart?* as a possible title for our last book to our female editor and agent.

Crickets.

I don't know which surprised me more, that we were deluded enough to think they'd like it, or that we were able to get the words out for laughing. We thought it was the best title ever and 100% true.

I never let my mom get away with a fart. I am the fart police. And we have five dogs, so my mom is often falsely accused. But in toots law, you're guilty until proven innocent, or in layman's terms, "the one who denied it, supplied it."

And like any good bro, I can dish it too. Not in real life—I would pass out before I allowed myself to pass gas in front of a friend or boyfriend—that's disgusting and rude. Unless I do it in front of my mom—then it's absolutely hilarious.

My mom and I also bond over football. Like a lot of guys, we have a baseline understanding of the sport—meaning we're low on stats, high on smack talk. It was my mother who raised me to be a proper Philly sports fan. That means you rag on the Eagles constantly, but you'd fight any out-of-towners who spoke against them. They are ours to hate, and ours alone.

We hate because we love.

I have this weird idea that my mom would be a great professional athlete, largely based on her ability to high-five. Her celebratory smacks feel like catching a fastball with your bare hand. At five-foot-two, she has the high five of LeBron James.

She will crush you.

After sports, another bastion of brohood is alcohol. Neither of us is a big drinker in our normal lives, but in recent years, whenever I'm home, my mom wants me to make us cocktails. She thinks that by virtue of living in New York City, I am now a certified professional bartender.

In reality, I only know how to make one drink really well, but it's the only drink you need: the margarita.

Tequila has a bad reputation, but like so many of us, it's just misunderstood. Forget shots, this spirit was made for sipping. I gave my mom a little education and now she's a tequila snob. She doesn't speak Spanish, but she knows the difference between *anjeo, blanco,* and *reposado,* and has opinions on each. Thankfully, we're on the same page that a true margarita has only three ingredients: tequila, triple sec, and fresh lime.

Don't even think about adding orange juice or sour mix in our house.

What is this, Mohegan Sun?

So we drink margs, catch the game, then watch *Role Models* again, and giggle if somebody burps.

How did we get this way?

Until a couple years ago, we didn't so much as have a male dog in the house. There were bras drying on the towel racks, Midol in the medicine chest, and a spare hair elastic in every drawer. It was all girls, all the time.

Maybe that's it. Maybe because for so long there was no man in the house, our sense of gender roles got softened. Or maybe those roles are just myths created by TV sitcoms anyway.

As they say, boys will be boys.

And sometimes, so will girls.

Motherhood Has No Expiration Date

· · · · · · · · · · · · · · ·

By Lisa

I have a scientific theory the bonds that tie mothers and daughters are love and worry, like the two strands in the double helix of some very twisty DNA.

In other words, if I love you, I worry about you. And vice versa.

Let me explain.

The moment Daughter Francesca was born, I started to love and worry about her. And my worry, like my love, had no bounds. I worried if she was sleeping too much. I worried if she was sleeping too little. Same with crying, nursing, and pooping. If I was breathing, I was loving, and worrying. And my biggest worry, of course, was whether she was breathing. I'm not the only mother who has watched her baby sleeping to see if her chest goes up and down.

I still do that.

My theory also applies to grandmothers. Because they're mothers, too. Just grander.

Mother Mary worried about Francesca, and all of our conversations back then were consumed with my worries and hers, and together we aimed our laser beams of worry on this hapless infant, which is undoubtedly why she turned out so great.

Or guilty.

Francesca knows we worried about her, uh, I mean, we loved her.

Likewise, I know, in turn, that Mother Mary worries about me. She worries that I work too hard. She worries when I fly. She worries when I drive. She worries when I'm not at home, and even more when I am at home. For example, she worries that I could put too much food on my fork and choke.

Let me suggest that this last worry isn't so dumb. You've never seen me eat.

I used to feel guilty that she worried about me, but now I don't.

She should worry about me, constantly.

It proves she loves me.

I realized this when I understood how much I still worried about Francesca even though she's living in New York, on her own. I don't mean to make her feel guilty, and she shouldn't. But I can't help it.

Motherhood has no expiration date.

And what just happened is that the worry has boomeranged, so that I'm starting to worry about Mother Mary.

Well, not starting.

But recently my worry, and my love, have come to the fore because of Mother Mary's health. In particular, her nose.

It's blue.

No joke. The last time she came to visit, the first thing that I noticed was that her nose had a distinctly bluish tinge. I told her so, in a nice way, and she told me to shut up.

But still, I worried, big-time. Her circulation has never been good, due to a lifetime of smoking, but she finally quit at age eighty-two, when she got throat cancer.

Better late than never.

Anyway, she beat the cancer, which is remarkable enough, but she's supposed to use oxygen at night, according to the doctor. But she won't do it. Our conversation today on the phone went like this:

"Ma, why won't you use your oxygen?"

"I don't like the tube. It smells like popcorn."

"So what? Popcorn is good. Who doesn't like popcorn?"

"I don't, and that's what it smells like, so forget it."

"But it's doctor's orders, Ma."

"Hmph! What does he know?"

I don't know where to begin. "Everything?"

But Mother Mary wouldn't listen even though I eventually raised my voice, which is another thing that mothers/daughters do to prove our love.

If I'm yelling at you, you know I love you.

Because I want your chest to keep going up and down, whether you're my daughter or my mother.

Or whether I'm your daughter or your mother.

It's all the same emotion, which is worry.

Or love!

So the next time your mother is worried about you, don't tell her to shut up.

And don't feel guilty either.

Try and understand. She can't help it. It's in her DNA.

Chalk it up to mom genes.

Ode to Vance Packard

By Lisa

Computer companies are full of great ideas, and I'm stealing one of them.

I'm selling my rough drafts.

Rather, uh, I won't think of them as rough drafts anymore. I'll think of them as earlier versions. I'll call them Scottoline 1.0.

Yes, that's right. I'm going to start selling unfinished things to make money.

Why not?

Granted, it won't be as good as the final product, but it'll be as good as I can make it in the time I took, and there's no reason not to sell it that way if people will buy it.

Dumb people, like me.

I bought two iPads at Christmas, one for Daughter Francesca and one for me, only to see Apple come out with the iPad 2.0, three months later. The new iPad has a camera and a better way of turning on and off. Why they couldn't have done this at Christmas, I don't know. Why they couldn't have *told* me at Christmas, I do know.

And so do you.

Apple makes fraud cool.

iFraud.

It's been doing this for so long that everybody accepts it as normal, and I'm not going to whine about it, herein. If you can't beat em, join 'em, right?

So I don't know why I have to wait until my sentence is in final draft to sell it. I don't know why I can't make it work for me, like this:

Today Mother Mary

In my opinion, it

Unlike Spanx, granny panties have been known to

My feet are so crusty they

Maybe I can sell my sentences the way they are above, even if they're unfinished and missing features.

Like verbs.

I could also sell them in draft form, so that they have all their features, but they're not really good enough, like this:

My feet are crusty enough to be pies.

Now if I worked on that a little more, I could come up with:

My feet are crusty enough to make pies jealous.

Now, that's pretty good. I like it better. I might even say it's final.

But only for now.

Until I think of a better sentence.

At least it has a verb, if not a camera.

Let's call that sentence Scottoline 3.0. We can agree that Scottoline 3.0 is the latest and greatest, and I could stick that sentence in a book and sell it, with a lot of other 3.0 sentences. But who's to say a Scottoline 2.0 sentence can't be sold as well, or even a Scottoline 1.0 sentence?

Especially if I put it in a white case.

This way I get people to pay for my rough drafts, and since I do about ten drafts a book, I can make Money 1.0, Money 2.0, and all the way to Money 10.0.

Ten times the amount of money.

I could be iFilthyRich.

If people think I'm being greedy, I'll explain to them that, no, on the contrary, it's just that I've never really finished anything, on account of my being an Innovator in a Relentless Quest For Perfection.

iScottoline.

By the way, Apple wasn't the first company to come up with this genius marketing idea. Back before computers even existed, car companies in Detroit would change their models every year, making the earlier version look dated, in what was called planned obsolescence. Reporters and consumer advocates railed against it, and everybody thought it was evil.

Those days are over.

That idea became obsolete.

Evil didn't.

Evil just dressed better.

Back in those days, in 1960, an author named Vance Packard wrote a book called *The Waste Makers,* which took American business to task for spending millions in advertising to convince people to buy expensive products and throw them away prematurely, when they'd become unfashionable. He thought this practice made American society wasteful, debt-ridden, and generally discontent, as we grew unhappy with what we had, because it wasn't the hot new thing.

I don't know what he's talking about.

That has no resonance today.

At all.

And so I'll keep my old iPad, though I'll be cranky about it, you bet.

The happy ending is that Francesca has been so busy since Christmas, she hadn't opened her iPad, so now we're going to take it back to the store and trade it in for an iPad 2.0.

Gotcha, Apple.

iPayback.

Cushy

· · · · · · · · · · · · · · · ·

By Lisa

This couch potato is getting a new couch, and it's harder than you think. I've chosen the wrong couch before, in my life. In fact, my couch mistakes rival my marital mistakes, though my couches have lasted longer than my marriages.

I'm not only unlucky in love, I'm unlucky in lounge.

We begin back in the Dark Ages.

In other words, my marriage to Thing Two.

When one of us had the great idea that not everything in the family room needed to match, so we acquired a red plaid couch, a floral chair, and a green-patterned chair-and-a-half. For those not in the know, a chair-and-a-half is just what it sounds like, big enough to accommodate dogs, laptops, and a double-wide tush.

That would be Ruby The Crazy Corgi's.

Anyway, the bottom line was that none of the furniture looked like it belonged together. Thing Two thought it was sophisticated, and he might have been right about that. Only problem was, I'm not sophisticated. I thought the furniture was too smart by half, especially the chair-and-a-half.

If you follow.

I thought things should have something in common if they were going to live together.

The same is true of furniture.

As soon as I was on my own again, I vowed to remarry wisely, that is, to get myself a couch and two chairs that matched. Yes, it's true, I'm "matchy-matchy."

I like to keep it simple. To me, that's how you know how things belong together. They look alike. So I reupholstered the furniture in a lovely gold honeycomb fabric, and I saved money by not buying new furniture. This was good financial planning, as it enabled me to afford the divorce, which was worth every penny.

But then the dogs took their toll, and the couch and chairs started to pop threads and look shabby. I liked the fabric so much that I had the couch and chairs reupholstered again, in the exact same fabric. You would think I'd move on and find a new fabric, but I wasn't ready to love again.

I yearned to commit to my couch.

But that was five years ago, and more dogs took their toll, and I decided it was time to get a whole new couch and chairs.

Of course, you may be wondering why I keep letting the dogs on the couch, and the reason is simple. If I didn't let the dogs up, how else would the ticks get on the couch?

So you see.

Which brings me to this morning, when I found myself in the furniture store, trying to decide between a bewildering array of fabrics: damask, tapestry, Jacobean print, plaid, patterned, bagatelle, and chintz. I also found my old honeycomb fabric in case I wanted to use it yet again, which is like ex sex.

I spent two hours there and still didn't know which fabric to pick, so I brought home a stack of swatches and arrayed them on the couch and chairs.

My method of choosing?

See which one Peach sat on. She's my Cavalier King Charles Spaniel, and she has the best taste.

She chose a yellow-and-pink chintz, but her compadre, Little Tony, liked the gold linen covered with birds that looked vaguely annoyed.

Angry Birds.

I didn't know which to choose.

And if you're wondering about price, they're both the same, which is costly. Oddly, chintz is not chintzy.

By the way, I didn't bring home a swatch of print fabric covered with Cavalier King Charles Spaniels. If I had, there would be Cavalier King Charles Spaniels sitting on Cavalier King Charles Spaniels, and I'd be certifiable.

Also, Ruby would be so pissed.

So my choice was between Angry Birds and Not-So-Chintzy Chintz.

The Angry Birds was lovely and classy, but I was partial to the chintz, despite the saleswoman's warning that chintz wears badly because it has so few "rubbings."

"What's a rubbing?" I asked.

"Rubbings are how many times your body can rub against the fabric before it wears out."

I lifted an eyebrow. "Who's rubbing their bodies on their couch?"

She blinked. "I don't know. I'm just saying."

I bit my tongue.

I'm going with the chintz.

If I want to rub my couch threadbare, it's my business.

Field Guide to the American Male

•••••••••••••••••

By Francesca

As a young nerd growing up, I used to love to read field guides. I owned field guides to insects, snakes, wildflowers, Hawaiian tropical fish, and North American songbirds. I had a collection of breed encyclopedias as well, including several on dogs, horses, and cats—wild *and* domestic. I loved the books' floppy faux-leather covers and the rows of glossy photographs, but what I really loved were the names.

Imagination is overrated—give me Latin classification any day!

It's a miracle I had any friends.

In high school biology, I remember learning about taxonomy, the science of classifying organisms, and how my teacher stressed the importance of proper nomenclature. Taxonomists estimate we've cataloged around 2 million species of animals so far, but that there remain between 3 and 100 million more species yet to be discovered.

Similarly, there are 8 million people in New York City, roughly half of them men. And I've only discovered about . . . well, that's private. The point is, well-organized classification is the first step to understanding. So I carry my very own field guide in my pocket every day:

My cell phone contacts list.

My contacts list has its own system of nomenclature. When I meet a guy in the field, so to speak, I don't always learn his last name. That's not as sketchy as it sounds, if you think about it. It would be weird if we all introduced ourselves with our full name. It worked for James Bond, but so did wearing a tuxedo every day.

I feel awkward asking a man I just met for his last name. It screams, "I'm going to Google you later."

I prefer to be discreet with my stalking.

Researchers in the field frequently work with limited information, but still, everything must be recorded. So I've developed a method of classification for these instances. I'm scanning my phone right now for an example . . . aha!

Aaron McManus.

Looks like an average name, right? But to my studied eye, I know that that entry is "Aaron," a guy I met at McManus, a local pub.

The formula is: First Name, Location of Discovery.

Entries like this are sprinkled throughout my contacts, forming a little scavenger hunt through my usual haunts.

There's Tony Pomme Frites, which sounds like a French mobster, but in fact, Pomme Frites is a restaurant that sells only fries and is open until 3:30 A.M. on weekends. I recall he complimented my shoes, we talked during the endless line, and I never saw him again.

Fries are bad for you anyway.

I also see the recently added, John Grassroots. Grassroots is a bar in the East Village. We met on a Friday, he called me on Monday, and I'm excited to see him this Thursday!

Mr. Grassroots has potential. If we have a nice time on Thursday, and I see him again, then he can earn a proper classification. But if it doesn't pan out, he'll languish in my contacts list, sandwiched between layers of G last names, frozen in time with the cute smile and the Ray Bans tucked on his shirt collar. A Contact Fossil.

My system is mainly designed to help me remember people when I pick up the phone, but sometimes it reminds me when *not* to pick up. A few examples:

Lucky Never. This guy works for my building-management company, but that didn't stop him from hitting on me outside my apartment. After I'd introduced myself, he actually winked and said, "You can call me, 'Lucky.'" I smiled, but what I wanted to say was, "You can call me never." Hence, his entry.

Roy Old Rusty Knot. Sadly, the name of the bar is only Rusty Knot. I feel a little bit bad about that one, but really, he was my father's age.

Creeper Noah. Ah, this is a special naming case. Normally, the first name is the most important information, but when it comes to creeps, the warning factor takes precedence. Also in my phone:

Creeper Josh.

Creepy Exterminator.

Unfortunately, my section C is packed.

Thank you, New York.

Boxers or Briefs

· · · · · · · · · · · · · · · · ·

By Lisa

I feel sorry for these men who are taking cell phone pictures of their privates and emailing them to women.

Say cheesy.

Some of these guys are taking the photos in their underwear, and some go commando, showing their sheaths unsheathed.

Yikes.

It started with a quarterback and spread to a politician, and now I'm kicking myself. If I had said something earlier, all of this foolishness could have been prevented. Faces could have been saved.

Not to mention, well, you know what else.

Somebody has to speak up, and it might as well be me.

The problem isn't that men are taking these pictures, or even that they're sending them to women they want to seduce. The problem is that these guys aren't going to get from Point A to Point B this way.

They need to keep their points to themselves.

(Sorry.)

Why? Gentlemen, take it from me, and I'm speaking for my entire gender:

No woman thinks this is your best feature.

Keep it in your pants.

We're not seduced by photos of your junk.

Call 1-800-GOT-JUNK.

They're called privates for a reason.

If we loved the way they look, they'd be called shoes.

Ladies, am I right or am I right? I know I'm going out on a limb. You can say you don't agree, especially if your husband or boyfriend asks, or is watching you read this. I get that. You love the guy. But get real. This is just between us, and we're talking turkey.

In fact, even a turkey is better-looking, and have you ever *seen* a turkey?

I know.

I'm betting my ovaries that we're all on the same page. These photos don't drive us wild. We've all been to the zoo, and nobody's turned on in the monkey house.

Except the monkeys.

I read in a scientific study that women aren't as visual as men when it comes to sexual arousal, but I don't think that's true. Maybe the women in the study weren't shown the right visual. Or maybe the scientists didn't show the visual to the right women.

Like me.

A cell phone photo of occupied tightie-whities doesn't do it for me, but I'd sit up and pay attention if a man sent me a photo of his abs, his shoulders, or his chocolate cake.

Break me off a piece of that.

And I admit, I enjoy the Bowflex commercials.

Oh yes.

The last Bowflex commercial I saw said that the machine uses "resistance technology." It sure does. And I can't resist.

When those arms curl, so do my toes.

Bowflex is the one commercial I don't fast-forward through. But I don't replay them. That would be pervy.

And women can also get turned on by the way a man looks, in general. We all know how I feel about George Clooney, and it ain't because of his brain.

So much for that women-don't-like-visuals theory. We're not blind, people.

And there are plenty of women who get turned on by less conventionally sexy body parts. Patrick Dempsey got called Mc-Dreamy because of his wavy hair. Jude Law built a career on his blue eyes. I myself have the hots for Mario Batali because he's chubby. It proves he can cook great food.

For me.

But visuals are a tricky business, and evidently it can't be left to quarterbacks and senators to decide which cell phone photos to send. If men are trying to get a woman interested, they should forget the picture-taking and use the cell phone the way God intended.

Call us.

And talk.

Say words.

Which words?

Tell us we're beautiful. Say that you're thinking of us. Offer to paint our house.

Or if a man is too shy to call, he should text something. I'd be totally turned on by a text that read:

SEE YOU TOMORROW TO TAKE OUT YOUR TRASH.

Yowsa.

Tickle

• • • • • • • • • • • • • • • •

By Lisa

They say that if you lie down with dogs, you wake up with fleas, but they're wrong. If you lie down with dogs, you wake up with ticks.

The other day, I fell asleep with Little Tony and Peach, and I woke up with a tick on my chin, like a mole. It works for Cindy Crawford, but not for me. I'll never get a date if I wear bugs.

I ran yelping to the bathroom, where I took off my nightgown and found another tick on my back.

Don't ask me how it got under my nightgown.

Obviously, ticks find me superhot.

The ticks were big, brown, and ugly, so I went online to look up what kind of ticks they were and found a webpage you don't want to look at for too long. I decided my ticks weren't deer ticks, but American dog ticks.

Which plague American dogs.

And American women.

My ticks look like bedbugs, only I'm the mattress, and I'm pretty sure they have three thousand legs, which are always in constant motion.

Creepy!

I don't know how they get anywhere, given that their legs seem to carry them in all directions, like a living Roomba.

Doing the Rumba.

The problem is Little Tony, a spaniel the color of a black bean. At any given time, he's giving a ride to three black ticks, none of whom tip well. I brush and inspect him all the time, but the ticks run and hide.

Never get a black dog. It's worse than a white rug.

I don't know if you can get Lyme's Disease from an American dog tick, but you can get the heebie-jeebies. So I went online and ordered a gross of Frontline, a goop that you put on dogs and cats to prevent ticks. Unfortunately, they don't sell goop you can put on humans to prevent ticks.

I'm guessing that common sense is the answer, as in, don't sleep with dogs.

Too late.

I actually have a little staircase at the foot of my bed for the dogs to use, but they don't use it.

The ticks do.

Frontline generally works well, but each package costs a hundred bucks, and with six critters at home, I can do the math.

It takes a second mortgage to keep me mole-free.

But the Frontline won't come in the mail for three days and until then, I can't sleep. On Day 1, I brush the dogs before we go to bed, but it doesn't put my mind at ease. I turn on the light at least five times to check Tony and find more ticks, so I spend the rest of the night imagining ticks walking all over me, getting under my clothing when they hadn't even bought me dinner.

In fact, to a tick, I'm dinner.

I was up all night, obsessed with ticks and watching the clock.

Tick tock.

See what I mean?

I didn't know when or where they'd appear next, and the constant worry rendered me sleepless. Ticks are the terrorists of the bug world, and the creepiest part is that they can crawl into various orifices. If you're a woman, you know what I mean.

Your ear.

A moth got caught in my ear last year, and it still creeps me out.

On Day 2, I get the dogs shaved at the vet, then brush them before bed, but, between two and five o'clock in the morning, I find four ticks, three on the dogs and one on my shoulder.

To me, it's the Night of a Thousand Ticks.

On Day 3, I shower and dress for bed like a beekeeper. Yet I still can't sleep, and on my last trip to the bathroom to check myself, I find yet another tick.

On my thigh, heading north.

And I'm at the pet store the next morning, buying Frontline.

In case one of the ticks has GPS.

iBurglars

. . . .

By Francesca

It took me over an hour to realize my apartment had been burglarized. So much for being a mystery writer's daughter.

Friday night, I came home late with my friend, Katy, who was visiting. Laughing with her, it barely registered that the lock didn't *click* when I turned the key. We flopped on the couch and reviewed our night, and it wasn't until I went to change into my PJs that I noticed my bedroom was a mess—well, more of a mess.

Then I saw the open window.

My computer was not on my desk.

I rushed to tell Katy. "I've been robbed. I need to call the police."

"Wait. Maybe you should call your mom first."

"Shouldn't I call the police first? That's more important, right?"

Katy bit her lip. She's been my best friend for fifteen years. She knows my mother very well.

I dialed my mom's cell. Without letting her get a word or a worry in edgewise, I told her, "Hi, Mom, I'm totally fine, but my apartment was broken into, so I'm calling the police. Everything's under control. I love you, bye."

Then I dialed 911.

Waiting for the police, I assessed what was missing: my Mac-Book Pro, its power cord, my iPad, and a totebag, presumably to carry the loot. My jewelry and wallet were untouched; they only took Apple products.

iBurglars.

Adding insult to injury, the stolen bag was a promotional tote for *Look Again,* by Lisa Scottoline.

When I told my mom this detail later, she said, "Maybe we'll get some readers out of it."

I imagine they'll make *Look Again* their next thug-book-club pick:

"The question is, guys, what really makes a mother?"

"Love, of course."

"And bail money."

Soon, two policemen arrived and took me through the standard questions and paperwork. A forensics team would have to dust for fingerprints, but due to high weekend demand, they couldn't come for three hours. The police said they'd wait with me. Even a rookie like me deduced coffee was in order.

With no respect for authority, my dog, Pip, jumped on one officer's leg for attention. "The dog was here when it happened?" he asked, patting Pip.

"Yes." I rounded the corner to the kitchen, still within earshot.

"I'm surprised they hit a place with a dog."

"He's not much of a watchdog," I called to them. "I'm just glad they didn't hurt him."

"Yeah, you're lucky. Last week—"

"Nmm-mm," Katy interrupted. I heard her say, "Don't. It will upset her."

May we all be blessed with a friend who will shush a police officer to spare your nerves.

If you are neither the victim nor perpetrator of a serious

crime, hanging out with the police is fun! They entertained us with stories of streakers on Seventh Avenue, "The Naked Highway." They dished department gossip on the crazy girlfriend who faked a mugging to get attention from her cop boyfriend.

I also learned that both officers were veterans of Iraq. Each showed me cell phone pictures of their pets—one had a cute rescued pit bull, the other a pair of beloved Ragdoll cats. The cat lover told me how he and his wife were in the process of adopting a baby, a lifelong dream of theirs, having both been happily adopted themselves.

By the time the sun came up, we were old friends.

"Can I make you guys some breakfast?" I asked.

Eyebrows lifted. "What do you have?"

"I have girl food—Greek yogurt, low-glycemic bread, vegetarian sausage. But I have eggs—real ones!"

They used their right to remain silent.

It was six o'clock in the morning when the forensics team arrived. In no time, they dusted, found nothing, and left in a puff of black mercury dust. Sadly, the time had come to say goodbye to my new police friends.

"You be careful now," said one.

"Get bars on that window," said the other.

I promised I would and thanked them again.

As scary as the ordeal was, I felt grateful. I was grateful the burglars had only taken things and not harmed my precious Pip. I was grateful Katy was there with me. I was grateful the police were so kind and professional, but not too professional to hug me goodbye. I was even grateful the forensics team took so long, since it afforded me the company of two of New York's Finest, to sit and chat until I wasn't afraid anymore.

It's dangerous to be alone in the city.

I'm lucky I'm not.

Homebodies

●●●●●●●●●●●●●●●●●●

By Lisa

I was apartment-shopping with Daughter Francesca when I realized that the sort of apartment that appeals to a mom is a lot different from the one that appeals to a daughter.

Here is what she wants: pretty.

Here is what I want: security.

Here is what she wants: charm.

Here is what I want: a doorman.

Here is what she wants: sunlight.

Here is what I want: a moat.

Uh-oh.

I thought we needed a better-managed building, and we rent an apartment together. She lives in it all the time, and I use it when I go to New York to see the opera or on business. To be honest, I don't have tons of "business" in New York. By "business," I mean "make up excuses to see my kid."

Not monkey business, mother business.

Hotels in Manhattan are crazy expensive, and I like to check Francesca out without checking in, if you follow.

What I do is trump up some afternoon meeting with my publisher, or whoever else will meet with me. Sometimes, nobody will. In fact, the next time you're in the city, let me know.

I'll meet with you. Then I'll use the meeting as an excuse to spend three days with Francesca, spying.

I mean, er, visiting.

That's the thing about kids. They can run, but they can't hide. And sometimes, they can't even run. Francesca is fast, but she's not fast enough. I'm the Runaway Bunny of Mothers.

Call it being a good mom.

Or stalking.

Either way, we found ourselves in New York, standing inside a perfect box of an apartment, located in a perfect box of a building, situated behind a fence of wrought iron topped with sharp points.

For impaling bad guys.

If you saw *The Omen,* you knew that already.

Plus it had a doorman with a desk, and hopefully, an automatic weapon.

In other words, Mommy wanted to sign the lease, but daughter was less eager. "It's not charming," she said.

"The doorman is charming," said I. "And a good shot."

"Don't you think the apartment is kind of . . . corporate?"

"Absolutely. Your point is?"

Francesca looked around at the other residents. "There's not many people my age."

Of course she was right about that. The place could have qualified as a retirement home, which appealed to me immediately as I intend to retire any year now, though that year has recently been pushed back to 3017.

Still, I preferred to accentuate the positive, so I told her, "Think of it as having a lot of substitute mothers. If you ever have a question about whether to preheat the oven, you can ask almost anyone."

Francesca was still frowning. "And it's kind of expensive."

"True, but you're worth every penny, and I won't have another daughter. The shop's closed, as you may know."

She looks unamused.

"No go, huh?"

"It's the prettiest office I ever saw."

I understand her point of view, secretly. When I was her age, I probably wanted all the things she wants, but I don't remember back that far.

So we walked a few blocks east and found ourselves standing inside a second apartment, a dressed-down affair with exposed brick and its own counterculture courtyard, complete with colorful Tibetan prayer flags. I know they're Tibetan prayer flags because I saw them once in a movie with Brad Pitt.

I myself am praying for Brad Pitt.

Anyway, back at the second apartment, guitar music wafts through the air, from a resident hippie, and the bedroom has a skylight that blasts sun everywhere.

"Yuck," I say.

Francesca turns around, surprised. "Ma, this place is great!"

"You can't sleep with all that horrible brightness. Also somebody could come through the skylight."

"Like Spider-Man?"

I sense she isn't taking me seriously, though I get it. The sagging floorboards, the gloppy paint job, and the crooked windowsills add up to character, and the only good thing about character is that it costs less.

I know this because I'm back in our current character-filled apartment, which is cheaper, and I'm parked sweating in front of a fan.

Character doesn't have central air.

But I will, in 3017.

Once Upon a Time

By Lisa

Even a week later, I'm still excited about the royal wedding. Go ahead, judge me.

I watch the reruns on the cable channels, and I bet I'm not alone. Menopausal women and ten-year-old girls are glued to those shows. They're like the best episode ever of *Say Yes to the Dress,* plus a kingdom and a cool blue sports car.

What's not to like?

I got a hot flash when the royal couple said their vows, which I guess is called a Royal Flush.

And now I talk about the royal wedding so much, I've become a royal pain in the you-know-what.

But it's understandable, isn't it? It's an historic event. Kate Middleton went from commoner to princess, and she did it with her natural hair color.

How do you swing that?

I thought fairy tales didn't come true, but they do. At least, sometimes. Kate kissed a frog, and he turned into a prince. I kissed a frog, and he turned into a jerk.

But I have hope.

I could become a princess, too.

If Prince William takes after his father, he's already in the market for an older, less attractive bride.

Me!

I was in New York at the time of the wedding, so Daughter Francesca and I got up at the crack of dawn and watched it, live. She made real scones from scratch, and I wore a tiara. The dogs slept through the entire ceremony.

They knew they'd catch it on rerun.

Or they thought that the wedding of two complete strangers, taking place an ocean away, simply had no relevance to them.

Silly.

What do dogs know?

(Answer: Everything.)

If you're wondering where I got the tiara, it was in Greenwich Village, where Francesca and I found a store called Fantasy World. We thought it was a costume store, because its windows had mannequins dressed in witch and cop outfits.

We didn't notice that the witch's costume came with fishnets.

Or that the cop's came with extra handcuffs.

It didn't register at first that it was strange for the store to be open at eleven o'clock at night. And full of men.

Also it wasn't Halloween.

We went to the desk and asked the clerk, "Do you have any tiaras?"

And she asked us, "With penises?"

I'm not kidding.

This was verbatim. I exaggerate all the time, but Francesca never does, and she'll back me up. And that's when we realized that we weren't in a normal costume store, but some kind of sex-costume store.

Yes, there are people who wear costumes for sex.

I'm guessing they all live in New York.

My advice? Stay home.

Evidently, they dress up as slutty cops, firefighters, nurses, doctors, and dentists. In Fantasy World, nobody's unemployed.

That's why it's a fantasy.

Maybe that's what gets these people excited. Their paycheck is on the way.

There's no aphrodisiac like being able to pay the bills.

But that's just me, and what do I know? I never dressed up to have sex. I dressed down.

Maybe that's where I went wrong.

Okay, I dressed up as a wife, but I gather that's not as sexy as dressing up as a witch. Of course, I've been called a witch, and that's kind of confusing. I must've been a bad witch, instead of a good witch.

Or maybe it was the other way around.

Anyway, back to tiaras. Kate Middleton wore the Cartier "Halo" tiara, made of platinum and diamonds. It dates back to 1936 and is priceless.

I wore the Scottoline "PG-rated" tiara, which was fake-platinum, with pink rhinestone letters that read BRIDE-TO-BE. It was made in China and cost $5.99.

You don't want to know what the penis tiara looks like.

Or maybe you do, but I'm not telling.

Moving On

· · · · · · · · · · · · · · · ·

By Lisa

I'm helping Daughter Francesca move, but we're going no-where.

Why?

Because we fight.

The trouble is the difference in our approach.

To everything.

And of course, we're adamant. We get that from Mother Mary.

When in doubt, blame it on your mother.

Unless your mother is me.

We begin with a basic difference to moving, in general. My approach is that everything in one apartment has to be put in boxes to be carted to another apartment, there to be unpacked. By the way, what I've learned is that if you live in New York, you essentially live in a box, so you pack a box to move to a box.

Some people move to bigger boxes, like from a matchbox to a ring box. Rich people live in an earring box. Only Donald Trump has a shoebox.

Francesca isn't moving to a bigger box, she's moving to a safer box, which is fine by me.

Since everything has to be unpacked, I don't think it mat-ters how it gets packed, which box it goes in, how much tape it has, or how the box is labeled. So I don't spend a lot of time on these details. I drive to New York and start putting things in boxes. It's not rocket science. Any one of my dogs can do it, and if I had my way, I'd hand them a roll of tape and tell them to get cracking.

So, for example, if I see a stack of dishes I put them in the box and tape up the box. On the box I write KITCHEN.

You see my logic.

It's like when you eat dinner. Does it matter whether you have the peas or the potatoes first?

Exactly.

To me, moving is like Thanksgiving dinner, with packing tape.

It doesn't matter what it is, only where it goes, and it all goes to the same place. And when it gets there and somebody un-wraps it, it will be a fun little surprise. Like Christmas morn-ing, only with things you don't want.

A spatula? For me? How did you know?

See how much fun I am? Every day is a holiday with me. That's why I'm divorced twice.

It takes me five seconds to pack a box, and if I packed the entire apartment, I'd have it done in fifteen minutes.

I think I'm doing great until I notice that Francesca is wrap-ping each dish individually with white paper and putting it in a box, then wrapping the entire wrapped stack with more white paper, then putting it in a box and stuffing the sides of the box with even more white paper.

"That's a lot of paper," I say.

"I don't want them to break."

"They won't break. We're only going three blocks away."

"Still. How are you doing it?" Francesca looks over, and I push the dogs in front so she can't see my bare little plate stack, like pancakes without the syrup.

Suffice it to say that words are exchanged. Many words, in a fight that takes longer than packing ten boxes. Especially the way that I pack them. In fact, the fight ends up being about the fight, which is our favorite thing. We fight over who said what in the fight, and especially the tone that was used.

Tone is the enemy of the mother-daughter relationship.

Also eye-rolling.

By the way, if you were thinking that it's Francesca who does the eye-rolling, you're wrong.

It's me. Guilty as charged. I'm a professional. I can roll my eyes, flutter my lids, and use the wrong tone all at the same time, which is a great example of multitasking by mothers.

Anyway, we resolve our argument by agreeing that I stop packing.

Fine with me.

Heh-heh.

There's cleaning to be done, so I volunteer to go clean the refrigerator. She wraps, and I clean, and when I'm finished, we make up, all nice. Kisses and hugs and tears.

And she says: "Where's the food from the refrigerator?"

I blink. "I threw it away."

"What? Why?"

"You wanted me to pack half jars of strawberry jelly?"

"Of course. It's only three blocks away."

"Aha! Why does it matter for the jelly but not for the dishes?"

And we're off and running.

Advertise Here

· · · · · · · · · · · · · · · · ·

By Lisa

I just saw one of those new electronic billboards, and it advertised a bank, then switched to a wanted poster for a bank robber.

I swear, I'm not making this up.

This would be a full-service billboard.

Or, taken together, it's an ad for where not to put your money.

This must be a new thing, putting bad guys on billboards. Driving to New York alone, I passed two billboards showing scary people wanted for murder. Their larger-than-life eyes glared at me as I drove by, and I hit the gas.

Yikes.

It's like Lite-Brite, the Felon Edition.

I decided that all murderers look alike. Generally terrifying, with bad hair. But don't tell them I said so.

For obvious reasons.

In the good old days, the bad guys were on the streets. Now they're in the skies, staring down at us, and I'm not sure this is progress. I like my crooks eye level, so I can run away. If they get in my head, there's no escape.

The geniuses among you will think immediately of Dr. T. J. Eckleburg, glowering from the faded billboard in *The Great Gatsby*.

The rest of you will look it up on Wikipedia.

But everybody's welcome here.

Read on, literati.

I know we're trying to catch bad guys, so advertising them on billboards probably makes a lot of sense.

Still, I'm not a fan.

Hear me out.

Billboards get the imagination going. In a world where we can fast-forward, tweet, and check our email during TV commercials, the billboard is the last bastion of old-school advertising. And you know what? It works.

Assuming that you're not texting as you drive.

And I'm not. No joke.

I think it's dangerous, and I took the Oprah pledge not to do it. Oprah's the last person I want mad at me. She has superpowers.

Like Dr. T. J. Eckleburg.

So when I'm on the road, I read every billboard, and I remember them. I bet you do, too. If you drive the same route every day, you know the billboards.

Do you really want to know murderers?

I drove up to New York last weekend and it was all I could do to keep my eyes on the road, for reading the other billboards. I love the normal ones, with the shiny happy people selling us things, and I imagine myself as the gorgeous woman in the perfume ad or the energetic woman in the coffee ad.

Scottoline runs on Dunkin'.

That's the point of a billboard, to capture the imagination. The perfume ad makes me feel gorgeous, and the coffee ad makes me feel energetic, two things I'm distinctly not.

Yay, imagination!

For this reason, my favorite billboard advertises the lottery, which is now at $300 million, according to two billboards I passed on I-95. Those billboards don't have any pretty people to engage the imagination, but they don't need them.

They have money.

And they keep my imagination going for hours. My endorphins fire like crazy as I think about winning the lottery, from the moment I realize I have the winning number, then to calling Daughter Francesca and Mother Mary with the news, and then imagining all the things I'd buy, mainly a house in Lake Como, next to George Clooney.

So I could borrow some sugar.

Or lend him some.

For one night.

Of course, the lake interests me not at all. I can't even swim.

But I have a lot of sugar.

And I would buy more.

In fact, I would become a sugar baron, cornering the sugar market, and pretty soon, even Matt Damon would have to stop by.

It's a plan, right?

Anyway, these billboards with the bad guys scare me, all the way to New York. They make me think of bad things like murder, and I already spend a lot of time thinking about murder, because I write murder mysteries. I don't need to think about murder on the road. I need a murder break.

That's why I think about George and Matt and Brad.

Sugar, for the brain.

Insecurity Clearance

· · · · · · · · · · · · · · · · ·

By Francesca

I just moved into a new apartment. The new place is nicer than my old one in several ways, but the number one difference is my new building has a doorman. Even though my doorman is a normal security guard and not one of those white-gloved Plaza types, having a doorman makes me feel very fancy and grown-up.

More accurately, it makes me feel like I should be fancy and grown-up.

Don't hold your breath.

My first week here, the doorman gave me a sheet of paper with a big, blank grid on it—this was my security list. He explained that I needed to list every person who had permission to use the doorman's key to enter my apartment without me, and then return the form to him to keep in the Security Clearance binder.

This was the serious business of serious people. I took the paper with appropriate gravitas and told him I'd have it back to him as soon as possible.

Composing my list started out easily enough. The first person I listed was my mother. In the column designated "Dates/ Times Permitted," I wrote: "always."

Just don't tell her, okay?

Then I decided to put down my father next, because that seemed fair. I imagine being a mother to twins is very similar to being a child of divorce—we both know that every gift, perk, and opportunity must be perfectly duplicated or there's bound to be hair-pulling.

I tapped my pen, struggling to think of anyone else to include. Maybe it was dumb that my only key users lived out of state. A responsible adult would have an "in case of emergency" contact nearby. But what emergency would necessitate someone getting into my apartment without me? The super already had a key in case there was a building issue, like a leak or fire. I guess it's possible that some misfortune might befall me, and I'd wind up in the emergency room. I'd need someone to bring me a bra.

You know my family history.

So I added my close guy friend who lives down the block as my "in case of emergency" person.

I didn't tell him he's on bra duty.

That seemed to cover it. I felt good about my list.

Until I handed it to my doorman the next day.

"That's it?" he asked.

"Well, yeah," I said, suddenly self-conscious. Maybe it was babyish for me to list my parents . . .

"This can't be it. What about your cleaning lady? Dog walker?"

"*I'm* the cleaning lady and dog walker."

He laughed like I had made a joke.

He would have laughed even harder if he saw what a crummy job said cleaning lady was doing in my bedroom. He wouldn't give her a key either.

"What about a significant other? You want to put a boyfriend on here?"

"No boyfriend." My mouth was getting dry.

Sheesh, this guy was worse than my relatives. And while my mother wanted me to have a doorman to keep out criminals, I wanted one to keep out crazy ex-boyfriends.

Trust me, within every boyfriend is a crazy ex waiting to be born.

The one and only time I gave a boyfriend a key to my place ended in complete disaster. After we broke up, he'd let himself in to leave me apology notes and hate mail in equal measure. His parting gift was a shoebox with a note that read, "Please take your belongings so I never have to see you again." The box contained some loose bobby pins, a hair elastic, and a plastic earring without its mate.

Thank goodness we were able to settle out of court.

Still, I didn't want my doorman to think I can't get a date, so I fibbed and added, "No boyfriend that I'm ready to give a key to."

He winked. "Smart girl."

I nodded like the worldly-wise woman that I am not.

Instead, I'm the woman who makes misleading statements in order to validate her social life to a doorman.

I was still wondering if my phony face of maturity looked too constipated when he snorted. "This is the shortest list we have!"

He must have seen the sheepish look on my face because he followed it up with, "But this is good, tight, secure—like it should be. This is my kind of list."

That's right, my list is secure.

Unlike me.

Fawning

· · · · · · · · · · · · · · · · ·

By Lisa

It was an ordinary day until I found a fawn in the garage.

Don't worry, this has a happy ending.

Here's what happened. For fun and adventure, I ride Buddy The Pony with two girlfriends who also ride, Nan and Paula. Well, the three of us cowgirls had just come back from our ride, exhausted. We weren't exhausted because we ride so hard. We rarely trot and never canter, so what we do is sit on the horses's backs while we talk. But sometimes our horses wander far apart from each other, as we have little or no control over them, and rather than stop talking, we merely shout our entire conversation to each other, which can be exhausting.

We're women, and we call this exercise.

I don't know what the horses call it, and I'm not asking.

After the ride, I went home, then to the car, which is when I found the little fawn. It was as adorable as Bambi, and seemed weak but otherwise calm, curled up by my car tire. Its lovely black eyes glistened, fringed with eyelashes I could kill for, and it had cute little white spots on its back. Its legs were long and knobby, and it couldn't have weighed more than ten pounds. It looked at me, I looked at it, and then I did what any woman would do.

Lisa's surprise visitor

I called my girlfriends.

Nan and Paula came over, and we all stood in a menopausal semicircle, oohing, ahhing, and worrying about the little cartoon fawn.

"Mommy, can I keep him?" I asked, and it seemed like a great idea. I have only four dogs and two cats, which is thirty-five pets shy of hoarding.

Plus I have no deer.

I could understand not keeping it if I already had a deer, but I was fresh out. And to be honest, I love deer. I didn't mind when they ate my plants, since they were hungry and they lived here first, and after a while, I just stopped planting anything.

If you can't beat 'em, quit.

Also I remembered reading a Monty Roberts book about how he kept deer as pets. I bet he could even ride a deer if he

wanted. If I rode a deer, I would do it with my girlfriends and we would talk and talk and talk until we were exhausted.

But back to the story.

Paula works with her husband, who's a vet, and thank God, she knows a lot about animals. She said, "We should call in animal rescue and see what they think we should do."

Nan nodded. She used to raise goats, and she knows a lot about animals, too. She said, "Good idea. I have a number in my phone."

So I watched the little fawn and imagined making it my pet while they called all manner of rescue services, vets, and knowledgeable friends. I stood hoping nobody answered, so I could keep the deer. I was already thinking of names for my new pet. She was a girl, I could tell by her long eyelashes, which is how you know.

The obvious choice for a name was Bambi. I couldn't think of another name, except Thumper. The only original name I could think of was Fawn, and I guessed I could call her Fawn Hall, which is the type of joke that amuses me and fellow baby boomers and nobody else.

Paula and Nan hung up the phone, both having gotten excellent advice. We should try to give the fawn some water, and though I didn't have a baby bottle, I had a big syringe (without the needle) that I use for giving Buddy medicine. So Nan held the fawn while I gave her water from a syringe, and if you don't know I was lactating, you're new around here.

Then, per directions, we took her out to the woods, where the other deer live. The animal rescue people said to check on her later, and if she was gone, that meant she'd found another mother.

So we did, and she must have, because she was gone.

But I miss Fawn Hall Scottoline.

And if she comes back, I'll have her cradle ready.

Starry Starry Night

. . . .

By Lisa

I should have mentioned that Mother Mary is living with me for the summer. We're in Day 16, which is now a countdown, like the Iran hostage crisis.

I'm waiting for the cable company to rescue me.

Until they get cable to the cottage, Mother Mary watches TV at my house, with the volume on eighty-six. That's the highest number of the volume on my TV, and it's not a number you should know. It's like having a car that goes 130 miles an hour. You don't need to drive that fast.

Mother Mary does.

UNDERSTAND?

ALSO, ARE YOU GETTING UP?

So, here's what I've learned:

Matlock starred Andy Griffith, not Dick Van Dyke. I had previously thought they were the same person, but they're not.

There are still shows with laugh tracks, and Mother Mary loves every one.

The fake laughter on the laugh track of *Everybody Loves Raymond* erupts in bogus hilarity every thirty seconds, like manufactured waves at a water park. If you're trying to work while the show is on, let's say if you're a writer, you'll find yourself waiting for the next wave, like a dripping faucet.

And the joke will be on you.

Ha-ha.

If *House* is on, Mother Mary has already seen it. This is also true of *Seinfeld, Two and a Half Men,* and *Law & Order,* regardless of whether the victims were special.

Oddly, that's a good thing.

Mother Mary will watch only shows she's already seen. If you ask her why, she'll say, "DON'T QUESTION ME."

But you will, anyway.

Because YOU HAVE A HARD HEAD.

Last night, so she could see something new, I suggested that we rent a movie on TV. She likes comedies, and *The Hangover* was on, so we sat down to watch it together. If you think that a movie with profanity and nudity might not be appropriate for my mother, it's time you knew the truth.

As soon as the movie begins, she asks, "IS THAT A REAL TIGER?"

I answer, "YES."

Next question, "IS THAT A REAL BABY?"

"YES."

Third question, "IS THAT BABY REALLY CRYING?"

"NO. HOLLYWOOD WOULD NEVER MAKE A BABY CRY FOR MONEY."

"BUT IT LOOKS LIKE IT'S REALLY CRYING."

"THEY DO IT WITH SPECIAL EFFECTS," I tell her, because it's okay to lie to your mother if it will prevent a cardiac event.

She looks at me sideways. She's hard of hearing, but she's not stupid.

Ten minutes into the movie, it strikes me that *The Hangover* is not a great choice for her plot-wise, because she asks, "WHAT HAPPENED TO THAT GUY'S TOOTH? WHERE DID

THE CHICKEN COME FROM? WHY IS THAT GUY IN THE TRUNK NAKED?"

I want to say, "DON'T QUESTION ME."

But I answer, and we spend the remainder of the movie screaming questions and answers at each other, after which we're both exhausted, so we call my brother to have him FedEx her hearing aids.

Then it's time for bed, and it turns out that Mother Mary likes a beer before she goes to sleep. I have no problem with this. She survived throat cancer and The Depression, and if she wants a brewski before bedtime, it's fine with me. She drinks Bud Lime, the choice of frat boys everywhere, and that's okay too.

So we sit in blissful silence, petting the dogs while she drinks her beer, and I feel torn. I could let her sleep upstairs in my house, but then she wouldn't get used to sleeping in the cottage, which is right in my backyard. The time it takes her to drink the beer gives me a chance to think, and I decide I have to stick with the plan. So I get her into her lab coat, which you might remember from previous books is her favorite outfit, and walk her down to the cottage, holding her bony little hand so the dogs don't trip her. And she makes her way through the grass, which is wet and soaks her sandals, and there's a chill in the air, under a night full of stars.

I point them out, and she looks up and smiles agreeably, though she can't see a single one.

And I get her inside her cottage, turn on all the lights, and make sure she can lock the door from the inside, which she does. Through the window, she gives me a brave thumbs-up, like an octogenarian astronaut.

"LOVE YOU, MOM," I tell her.

She can't hear, but she knows what I said.

The Many Homes of Mother Mary

By Lisa

•••••••••••••••••

Mother Mary makes everything an adventure, even a trip to the food store. And by adventure, I mean fistfight.

We begin in the produce aisle, where she's looking for bean salad. There's a counter that contains all sorts of prepared salads, including a five-bean salad, but Mother Mary eyes it with disdain.

"No," she says simply.

"What's the matter with it? It has five beans. That's two more than anybody needs."

"It doesn't have pinto."

"What difference does that make?" I have no idea what a pinto bean even looks like. I thought a pinto was a car.

"I like pinto. I want pinto."

"Then add some," I say.

Mother Mary throws up her hands. "If I wanted to cook, I wouldn't come to the food store."

Fine. I always thought that people who go to food stores then go home to cook, but what do I know?

We move on to the tubs of chicken salad, and there's another problem. "No," she says again.

"Why?"

"Too busy."

I don't understand. Chicken salad isn't busy unless it's wearing plaid pants with a polka-dotted shirt. "It has celery and mayonnaise. What's busy?"

"Forget it." She looks around, her white head swiveling neatly as a snowy owl. "We need broccoli and cauliflower."

"I'm on it. You stay here." I leave her with the cart, run to the broccoli and bag it, then run to the cauliflower and bag it, and come back.

"No good."

"What?"

"I want broccoli and cauliflower together."

"I got it together." I hold up both bags, one in each hand. "See?"

"No, they have to be *together*. In Florida, they have broccoli and cauliflower in the same bag."

"No problem." I take the bag of cauliflower and stuff it in the bag of broccoli. "Welcome to Pennsylvania."

Mother Mary shakes her head. "At home, they have it in the same bag, cut up, and you cook it that way."

"Well, this is your home, too, and we can take it, cut it up, and cook it together."

She blinks. "This isn't my home."

"Yes, it is. You have your house here, and your house in Florida."

"Only one is home."

"We'll see about that." I sense we're not fighting about vegetables anymore, as I'm astute that way, and in the Scottoline household, almost anything can turn into a power struggle, including vegetables.

Even the cruciferous become crucibles, if you follow.

So we move on to a fight in the next aisle, where they don't carry Ensure, and to a fight in the aisle after that, where they don't carry Dial soap.

I don't see her problem. "Ma, what's the big deal with Dial?"

"It's laid, spelled backwards."

Oh.

I hurry her through the checkout counter, where I try to stuff her in a recyclable bag, but they stop me.

Just kidding.

We go home and have dinner together, and I put the broccoli and cauliflower in the same pot, overcooking them so that the cauliflower turns a cadaverous white and the broccoli takes on a gangrenous hue.

"Delicious," Mother Mary says with a smile.

"Pennsylvania's not so bad, eh?"

"Shut up," is all she says.

Mother Mary learns to love the outdoors . . . for a few minutes.

Mother Mary takes Peach and Little Tony for a spin.

Later, we clean up the dishes and she tells me that she misses our old cat Smoochie, who passed way.

"I have his ashes upstairs," I say, and she lifts a sparse gray eyebrow.

"Really?"

"Sure." I keep the ashes from all of my pets, for the past thirty years, in my office. The dogs Bear, Rosie, Bertie, Lucy, and Angie. Smoochie is the only cat, and I even have a chest of ashes from Francesca's horse, Joy. In case you were wondering, a chest of horse ashes is roughly the size of a footlocker, and now you know why I work in the kitchen.

So I tell her all of this, then add, "I want to be cremated, too. Put me in a little cedar chest and stick me on the shelf in my office."

"I don't want to be cremated."

"No?" I ask her, which is when I see her expression darken and realize that the conversation just took a serious turn. So I twist off the faucet and ask gently, "What do you want?"

"I want a mausoleum." She starts to smile, and so do I.

"Really?"

"Absolutely. At the food store, you said I have a house in Florida and a house in Pennsylvania. Well, I want another house. In Holy Cross."

I laugh. "You're not going out cheap, are you, Ma?"

"Hell, no," she answers, with a wink.

Happy Birthday

....

By Lisa

It's my birthday, and I'm spending it with Mother Mary, which I know is a gift.

But unfortunately, you can't return it.

Just kidding.

I've said that aging isn't for the fainthearted, but I was talking about turning fifty-five. Now that I'm fifty-six, I realize how right I was.

Older and wiser, that's me.

And living with Mother Mary, who's eighty-seven, I'm beginning to see what strength is all about.

No kidding.

Strength is trying to walk forward when you can barely see.

Strength is trying to change a channel when you can't find a button on the remote.

Strength is trying to open a jar when you can't grasp it properly.

Strength is trying to speak when you've been robbed of your abilities.

Strength is remembering how things used to be, but knowing they aren't that way anymore. And going ahead anyway.

She is strongest, though her body is weakest.

I'm not trying to be a downer. I know that many older people lead full, active lives, and I hope to be one of them. But I'm living with one older person in particular, who has survived two strokes, throat cancer, and the cancellation of *Law & Order*.

Being with Mother Mary has opened my eyes to the fact that life isn't easy if you're a senior, especially a *senior* senior.

Microwave buttons are hard to read. The stairs in a movie theater are tough in dim light. Large print books are hard to find. Menus, cans, and bottles are unreadable.

Why can't there be an earphone on a TV, so we don't have to TURN UP THE VOLUME?

And there are salespeople in the world who are patient with older people, but some who aren't. If anybody's going to be nasty to my mother, it better be me.

Can we accommodate seniors better? I'm not the only baby boomer to be asking this question, and I bet we all become very interested in the issue, the older we get. Or as more of us take in our relatives and see how very strong they have to be, in their own special way.

Living with her makes me realize that we worry about all the wrong things. I see women every day on TV, and in the market, whose lips look suspiciously plump, and I wish them luck. But when I see what Mother Mary is worrying about, it isn't her looks. I know this because I just replaced her thirty-year-old bra and had to wrestle her into a new one. Two women and four breasts, flailing about in a dressing room. It gives a new meaning to girl-on-girl action.

It's not about her wrinkles, it's about the very senses that enrich our lives and keep us in contact with the world around us. We discuss this over lunch, which she agrees to have outside, even though she hates bugs, because it's my birthday.

Francesca, Lisa, Mother Mary, Laura, and Franca celebrate
Lisa's birthday with a girls' night out.

"Happy birthday, honey!" she says, with a smile. Then,
"Wanna see the scar?"

I laugh, though I've heard it before. I was delivered by Cae-
sarean section, and for a joke, she would flash me her scar. That's
the walking lesson that is Mother Mary.

She gave birth, and it left a mark.

She bears the marks of all of her days, good and bad, and so
do we all, ultimately. We go forward with our failing eyes and

ears, our steps slowed and speech sometimes a little funky. But if we're lucky, we go on, knowing that life isn't what it was, but it's something new, and after all, it's life.

That alone is precious, and enough.

In the end, she's the Birthday Girl.

Aftershocked

· · · · · · · · · · · · · · · ·

By Francesca

Italian women are stereotypically over reactors. My mother, for example, makes nuclear reactors seem reasonable. But I pride myself on being the cool-headed one. I can win any argument, or at least whip my mom into a frenzy, simply by remaining calm. So I always imagined I'd perform well in an emergency. I finally got my test case in an East Coast earthquake

I was writing on my laptop, when all of a sudden I felt as if the floor was swinging. I thought it was in my head, maybe a migraine or caffeine overdose. But then I saw the ripples in my water glass, and if *Jurassic Park* taught me anything, it's that when that happens, it's time to get out of the jeep.

In the next moment, my TV started wobbling and my picture frames fell off the shelves. I had no idea what was happening, but I wasn't sticking around to find out. I leashed Pip, grabbed the keys, phone, snatched a pair of flip-flops, and flew down six flights of stairs barefoot, like a monkey down a tree.

I skidded outside on the sidewalk, bewildered and out of breath, only to find everyone else going on his or her merry way, oblivious. Excess adrenaline coursed through me, but there were no opportunities to be heroic—no child trapped beneath a car, no unconscious adult in need of a fireman's carry, not even a kitten in a tree. In fact, no one seemed concerned at all.

Fear made room for embarrassment, as I became aware that a) I was apparently the only person who had almost wet herself in the last minute, and b) I was not wearing a bra.

I'd like to say I was raised better than this, but the last time my mom went to the ER, she wasn't wearing a bra either. It's practically family tradition.

Pip, also unconcerned, pulled at the leash, so I crossed my arms and walked him around the block. The dog looked for spots in need of pee while I looked for anyone whose look of panic matched mine; Pip found several lucky lampposts before I found a single comrade-in-alarm.

There's a new restaurant under construction on the ground floor of the building next door. The head contractor always tries to chat me up when I walk by, so normally I avoid the corner, but when he greeted me today, I didn't let him get a word in.

"Hey, hey, hey. Guillermo, hey, it's Francesca, hi, c'mere." I tried to slow my speech, but after being struck dumb with fear, my tongue decided it was its turn to freak out. "Did you just feel anything, like, shaking?" I realized my hands were shaking, which I hoped he took as active storytelling. "Did you guys just bust out a wall, or drop anything heavy, or something?"

He shook his head.

"Oh, okay, because, well, this is gonna sound crazy—" I tried to toss off a laugh, but it missed casual by an octave and came out at loony-bin pitch. "But I swear the walls of my apartment just shook."

He frowned, looking a bit skeptical, so I threw in my trump card:

"A picture fell off the shelf!" The gravity of the statement diminished when I said it aloud.

"Well thanks for letting me know, I'll ask my guys," Guillermo said. "In case I find out anything, how about you give me your phone number?"

"Good thing one of us keeps calm in emergencies."

"Okay, good idea."

Yes, if you catch me in an emergency, I am this naive.

I had just handed the pen back to him, when my cellular service returned and a text message from my mom chimed in:

"U heard about earthquake in VA/DC? Aftershocks on E coast. Turn on TV. Love you!"

Finally, an explanation! But my next thought was for the victims in Virginia and D.C. Surely any earthquake whose after-shocks scared me so must have unleashed utter devastation at its center. Is the White House a pile of rubble?

Oh no? It's totally still there, really? Everybody pretty much a-okay, huh? Well, thank God! Glad to hear it.

So maybe I over-reacted a little. But it's not my fault.

I am the granddaughter of Mother Mary, once dubbed "Earthquake Mary" by *The Miami Herald,* because she was the only person in Miami to feel an earthquake that occurred four hundred miles away in Tampa.

You can't fight genetics.

Stroke, Stroke, Bail, Bail

· · · · · · · · · · · · · · · · ·

By Lisa

I don't know how to swim but that doesn't stop me from trying.

Let me explain.

I never learned how to swim, because it involves putting your head underwater, which is a problem for me, as I require oxygen to live.

Also I'm terribly nearsighted, so if I take my glasses off, which is the kind of thing people expect when you swim, I can't see the Atlantic.

When I was little, I would go stand at the water's edge and jump waves with my brother. I have recurrent nightmares of being drowned, which is either a residual memory of those days or a flashback to my second marriage.

You won't be surprised to know that Mother Mary can't swim, either. She always says that she has a deal with the sharks. She won't go in the water if they won't go on the land.

When we were little, she would go to the water's edge to watch us and make sure we were safe. That she couldn't swim didn't seem to matter.

We lived, so it must have worked.

I'm lucky enough to have a pool and I've been known to float around on an inflatable raft and fall asleep. I also do a lot of clinging to the side, like a girl barnacle. I hang on tight and walk myself around the pool, hand over hand, which is kind of like swimming on land.

But last week, when the temperature hit 100 degrees, I eyed my pool and told myself it was time to conquer my fear.

Putting on a bathing suit.

Just kidding.

I have no problem putting on a bathing suit. After all, no one else is around, and the dogs think I look superhot. They have great taste, even if they think cat poop is a meal.

So I went into the pool, stood in the shallow end, and decided to swim a lap. I wasn't sure how to go about it, as I lack gills, but I'd seen Penny do it a bunch of times. So I started paddling, my head above water, and all four paws flailing wildly.

Dear reader, I made it to the side. Gasping. Panting. Exhausted. But alive. Which only encouraged me to get Mother Mary into the act. Yes, she's still here, and no, I didn't use her for a raft.

It began with, "Ma, wanna come in the pool?"

And ended with "please please please."

But when the temperature hit 104 degrees and the power went out, including the air-conditioning, my nagging did the trick. She came to the pool with me and put her feet in. We sat on the side, me in a bathing suit and her in her tank top and shorts. Our feet dangled in the water, and she wears a size five-and-a-half shoe, which means that there are kittens with bigger feet.

"Feel cool?" I asked her.

"No. Feels wet."

"I paid extra for wet," I told her. "And look, no sharks."

"I don't like it."

In my last story about Mother Mary, the headline read, MOTHER MARY, WHY SO CONTRARY? I don't write the headlines, but I had to admit it was kinda true. "Mom, you say 'no' a lot, you know that?"

"No, I don't."

I thought about it then, looking at her tiny feet under the clear water. She's come a long way. She was the youngest of nineteen children and had a mother who wanted her to drop out of high school, go to work, and bring home her salary. But she insisted on graduating. In short, she said no.

And she still does.

"Ma, you don't have to go in the pool if you don't want to."

"Good. Let's go."

So I helped her to her feet and put her into her sneakers, and

This is as close to swimming as Mother Mary gets.

we walked to the house, hand in hand. "Swimming is overrated, anyway," I told her. "I know, I tried it."

"Don't do it again, without me there."

"I won't," I promised her. "You want salmon for dinner?"

"No," she said, and we went inside.

The Facts of Life

. . . .

By Lisa

You may not know that you can see a movie in closed-captioning, but I do, and it's all because of Mother Mary.

That it was the wrong movie to see in closed-captioning is entirely my fault.

We begin when I realize that she's getting bored. To be honest, I don't realize it at all until she tells me so, one day.

"I'm bored," she says.

This happens to be a pet peeve of mine, as I believe people have an obligation to busy their own minds, and whenever anybody says I'm bored, I always think:

Read a book.

Sing a song.

Go to the movies.

But I love my mother, and she has a good excuse for being bored, at eighty-seven. She can't read because of her eyes, and she can't sing because of her throat. That leaves one thing.

"Wanna go to the movies?" I ask her.

"Yes," she says.

I blink, surprised. "Yes? But you always say no."

"I know, but I heard from Cousin Nana that you wrote about it. So now I'm saying yes, for spite."

I take her to *Crazy, Stupid, Love* because she thinks Steve

Carrell is cute, and she has a blast. She smiles the whole time, rapt, at the screen, her hands held curiously in front of her, in a happy little ball. Her tiny white head is the brightest spot in the theater, and her feet don't touch the floor.

But she's the only one laughing at the wrong times.

I look over, puzzled. She has both of her hearing aids in, but she still can't hear. When we leave, I say, "Did you have fun?"

"I loved it! Let's go again."

"Okay, maybe next weekend."

"Can't we go tomorrow night?" She turns to me, hopeful as a toddler in a gift shop, and I can deny her nothing when she looks at me that way, which is never.

"Of course."

"I want to see that movie in the preview, with Justin Timberlake. He's cute."

"You mean *Friends with Benefits*?"

"That's the one!"

I hesitate. I don't know if she knows what the phrase means. Someday I'll tell her the facts of life. Maybe when she's older. "Ma, do you know what that movie's about?"

"Of course, they're shacking up."

So there you have it.

I go online and notice that *Friends with Benefits* is playing the very next night, at ten o'clock, in closed-captioning.

Dirty movies for the hearing-impaired.

Yay!

So we find ourselves in the theater, with six other people, all young couples, sitting around us. They're not there for the closed-captioning, they're there to make out, and they dig in, even before the movie starts. And there we are, mother and daughter, at the center of their R-rated action, like the calm eye of a sex hurricane.

In other words, we're seeing *Friends with Benefits*, with friends with benefits.

Mother Mary notices none of this. She awaits Justin Timberlake.

Actually, so do I.

The movie begins, and the captions come on, but they're not like closed-captioning on TV, which is small and at the bottom of the screen. They're mile-high letters that take up almost the entire screen and they're translucent, so you actually see through them to watch the movie.

I'm trying to get used to it when the PROFANITY begins, in HUGE LETTERS.

I can't print them herein, but this movie has at least twenty F-WORDS in the first five minutes, evidence of its screenwriters showing they're down with the demographic, except that the demographic is playing tongue hockey and the only people watching the movie are the postmenopausal.

And the postpostmenopausal.

And just when I'm getting used to that, the sex scenes begin, and I get to read MY NIPPLES ARE SENSITIVE, complete with nipples.

With my mother.

But she watches the movie with the same smile as the night before, her hands clutched in the same little ball, and she sees plenty of Justin Timberlake, even his naked butt. The screen reads TOUCH MY ASS.

"Great movie!" she says, afterwards.

"Did the captions help?"

"They were great!"

But she looks too happy to be talking about the captions.

THE END.

Southern Exposure

· · · · · · · · · · · · · · · · · ·

By Francesca

When I invited my stepsister up to the city to celebrate her twenty-sixth birthday, I thought I could show her all that New York has to offer—fantastic shopping, fine dining, and of course, the sights.

I didn't mean for us to get an eyeful.

We were walking our dogs after a great dinner, when a man stepped out from between two parked cars and faced us. Let's just say, he was not dressed for the weather.

"EW!" I shouted at full volume. "GET AWAY! YOU'RE DISGUSTING. BACK OFF BEFORE I MACE YOUR . . ."

You get the idea.

So did he. He zipped up and zipped out.

"Eyyucck!" I tried to physically shake the nasty image from my mind. "That makes me so mad. I'm sorry you had to see that."

My innocent birthday girl was still trying to process the full-frontal affront. "Was he, was that his . . . ?"

"Yes, and yes. Gross."

"You reacted so fast. I didn't even see it at first!"

"I know that guy."

"You *know him*?" Her eyes widened.

"No, I mean, he's flashed me before."

In fact, this was the third time I had seen more than I wanted to of this un-gentleman. Each time, I tried to respond in a way that would convey my readiness to wake everyone in the five boroughs if he took one more step toward me. And I wasn't kidding about the mace.

One time, after he flashed me and bolted, I spotted him again minutes later one block over, but this time, he didn't see me. I yelled at him from across the street, "I recognize you! Get out of here before I call the police!"

At least I think it was him.

It's harder to tell with his pants up.

So I'm an old pro with the perverts. Not only was this not my first time being flashed, this guy wasn't even my first flasher. The first one happened outside of an ultra-chic, expensive restaurant in my neighborhood. This place is so exclusive it has an unlisted number; you have to physically stop in and grovel to get a reservation. Unless, of course, you're one of the celebrities who frequent the it-spot—I've seen stars like Beyoncé, Madonna, Hugh Jackman, and repeat guest Salman Rushdie.

Unfortunately, the flasher was not Hugh Jackman. He couldn't sexually harass me if he tried. I'd consider any amount of Jackman nudity a public service.

Rushdie, not so much.

Instead, it was a member of the kitchen staff who, when I walked by with my dog late one night, decided to offer dinner *and* a show—a 2 A.M. show of him doing the hand jive, wearing his apron as a loincloth.

The next morning, I told my mother, who was visiting, what had happened. We were both angry and creeped out, and I said I intended to march over there and tell the management.

She supported the idea, adding, "Maybe we'll get a free meal out of it."

"Mom! I don't want to eat there now. That guy who did this works in the kitchen . . ."

I don't have to make the joke, do I?

"Oh, right." Still, my mother looked disappointed. Apparently star sightings are worth the risk of contamination.

To his credit, the manager was appropriately appalled and apologetic. I didn't even have to say, "What if this had happened to Beyoncé?!"

I'm sure he was already thinking it.

I never saw the naked chef again.

This other guy has been harder to shake, no pun intended.

It was only a couple weeks after the birthday incident when I saw the Repeat Offender again. I gave my usual response, with added exasperation:

"EW! That is SO RUDE! I do NOT want to see that!"

Only this time, I think I got through to him.

Not that he put his not-so-shy friend away. No, he remained exposed, but he moaned, "So-oo-rrr-ry."

And they say men can't apologize.

I stormed off, and he slunk back into the dark, but for the first time, we both left satisfied.

Wag the Technology

By Lisa

The dog is supposed to wag the tail, not the tail wag the dog, but somebody needs to tell this to technology.

We begin when Daughter Francesca comes home for the holidays, and we want to see a movie. Unfortunately, the movie is at 8:20 P.M., which means that if we go, we'll miss two of her favorite TV shows, *The Real Housewives of Beverly Hills* and *The Bachelor*.

And by her favorite, I mean my favorite.

I love trashy reality TV, but I never think of it that way. I try to find the deeper themes in these shows, but I'm pretty sure that's one of the lies I tell myself, like that it's not fattening to eat M&Ms after lunch, but it is after dinner.

Dinnertime is the line in the sand, carbs-wise.

"So what should we do?" I ask Francesca. "Go to the movie or stay home and watch TV?"

"We can do both." She picks up the remote. "I'll record the shows, and we'll go to the movie."

I'm not a rube, I know you can record TV shows, but I don't make a habit of it, because I'm not pro-active in general. If I missed the TV shows, I'd have lived with missing the TV shows. Everything happens for a reason, so maybe I was meant to miss *The Bachelor*.

Come to think of it, maybe we're all meant to miss *The Bachelor.*

And the typical reality TV show will repeat what happened in the previous segment at the beginning of each new one, like programming for people who lack short-term memory.

Or a frontal lobe.

I guess they do this so that new viewers can start watching the show at any point, but I don't know how many people have new viewers strolling into their family room every five minutes.

I don't know half that many people, and I wouldn't let them in if I did.

Or maybe it's because of people who change the channel a lot, but I generally can't be bothered to do that, either. When I watch TV, I vegetate. There are eggplants that change the channel more often.

Plus I can never find the remote. That's why I work so much at night. In my house, it's easier to write a novel than to find the remote.

Francesca and I went to the movie and got home at 11:30 P.M. Left to my own devices, I would have walked the dogs and gone to bed, but Francesca is a lot more fun than I am, so she had other ideas.

"Let's watch our shows," she said, going into the family room.

"Okay," said I, because I'm generally eager to act like I'm not dead yet, when I really am.

So there we were, both in our chairs, with Francesca clicking away on the remote to start the *Real Housewives* recording, hitting PLAY, then pressing buttons to speed through the commercials and even more buttons to replay parts we missed.

I watched her, figuring all that button-pressing probably used up enough calories to justify a few M&Ms, even after dinner.

But the net result was that we were up for the next two hours, trying to watch our shows. My eyelids got heavier and heavier, but I wouldn't let myself go to sleep, and I began to wonder when entertainment morphed into work.

Without the money part.

Francesca felt the same way. The night wore on, and even she got tired, but we decided we had to finish watching the shows or we'd have to get up early to watch them, since she was leaving the next morning. To me, it hung over my head, a chore that couldn't be ignored, like a pile of laundry to be folded or a sinkful of dirty dishes.

Okay, those I can ignore.

But a fresh ep of *The Bachelor*?

Please. I'm only human. And the world's oldest-living *Bachelorette.*

Somehow the TV shows had finagled their way onto my Things To Do list and gone straight to the top, simply by virtue of being recorded. Francesca and I were up watching TV until after one in the morning, and we were sleepy the next day.

It's all technology's fault.

Before I got a DVR, I got plenty of ZZZs.

But now the tail is wagging the dog, Francesca, and me.

Stay tuned.

Kicking Tuches

• • • • • • • • • • • • • • • •

By Francesca

On a lark, my friend and I decided to take an introductory class in Krav Maga. *Krav Maga* means "contact combat" in Hebrew, and it's comprised of the physical training and self-defense techniques developed by the Israeli National Army. It is a no-rules, no-holds-barred style of combat intended for street fighting.

Still, I don't think either of us was taking it too seriously. We like to work out together, so when the class was offered on an online sale site, we signed up. The morning of, we met up outside the building with our bouncy ponytails and a spring in our step, excited for our fitness adventure.

The studio was on the third floor, but taking an elevator to a fitness class seemed hypocritical, so we opted for the stairs.

By the first landing, we regretted our decision. The stairwell was dark, dirty, and industrial, lit by a crackling fluorescent light. It was as if the entrance had been designed to convince you that you need a self-defense course. You need one yesterday.

They should stage mock muggings around the corner to drum up business.

When we made it safely to the studio, our bravery was rewarded with a free T-shirt. A huge man with a very precise haircut was handing them out. I imagined they chose him for the job to deter women from asking to "see the small," when we all know we're a medium. Fortunately, all the sizes looked like baby clothes in his meaty paw.

"We got two colors, black or blue," he said.

I laughed. See, that's funny, because black-and-blue . . .

His stony affect indicated the pun was unintended. This guy seemed like the type for less wordplay, more gunplay.

I swallowed and took my shirt.

My friend and I sat in our matching blue T-shirts, giddy with nerves. I was surprised to see we were the only ones who hadn't chosen black.

Perhaps "baby blue" wasn't the best color to convey intimidation.

Excuse me for wanting to bring out my eyes during combat.

Two female instructors entered and introduced themselves. I was relieved they seemed more personable than the human-Cerberus guarding the T-shirts.

Within the first few minutes, I could tell these women were badass. They stood with their feet superhero-width apart. They said the F-word. They looked good in drawstring pants.

I was impressed.

In a quick demonstration, they morphed into Krav Maga Tasmanian Devils, a whirlwind of spinning and shouting and kneeing and grunting.

People who feel comfortable grunting in exertion fascinate me. That kind of confidence is like a superpower. Can they say, "I love you," first? Can they also poop at work?

I was already feeling empowered.

Until they started talking.

The best and worst thing about Krav Maga is that the instructors make no bones about the objective. Krav Maga is not treated as the "practice" of an "art," but a set of practical methods of hurting someone, or, as with this women's self-defense class, stopping someone from raping and/or killing you. This frankness makes the information both easy to understand and completely terrifying.

The instructor began describing the scenarios and attacks that we would address in the seminar. I listened as she outlined what to do if someone is a) choking you against a wall, b) choking you while forcing you backwards, or c) pushing you forward into a car or trunk.

As she spoke, I caught sight of my face in the mirror.

I looked like I was going to pee myself.

This was not the face of Krav Maga.

But then, as she described our defensive moves such as gouging his eyes, kneeing him in the "nut sack"—a technical term—ripping back his thumb, etc., I caught myself making the same pained grimace.

Feeling sorry for your hypothetical attacker: *so* not Krav Maga.

After we had learned the basic stances and practiced some defense moves on our own, we paired up for role-playing, acting out attacks and defenses in a slower, controlled way. Thank God I had a friend with me, because fighting with a total stranger would be awkward.

Or awesome, if you asked the one instructor who cried, "This is the only time you get to choke a total stranger for fun!"

In the first go-round, I played the choker and my friend was the chokee.

Let me tell you, it's extremely difficult to throttle someone, even pretending, and not make weird faces. I don't know how serial killers do it.

I discovered this when, instead of breaking my grip with a shoulder swing, then jabbing me in the face with her elbow, my friend was laughing at me.

"I'm sorry, but you're making a funny face," she said.

"That's my attacker face! I'm attacking you!"

"It's just so funny." She dissolved into giggles.

After sufficiently mocking me, she pulled herself together for another try. I approached her again, this time slowly placing my hands on her throat with a forcibly relaxed expression.

She didn't react at all.

I dropped my hands. "What now?"

"Oh, did we start? I didn't realize," she said. "Because you didn't make the face!"

We both cracked up.

Then the instructor made a general announcement, clearly pointed at us, about not talking during the exercise. It was just like high school, except this time, we obeyed.

No need to test her stance on corporal punishment.

The rest of our exercises went better: we were starting to get the hang of it, although we were the most polite sparring partners ever—"Shoot, I forgot to kick you in the balls that time, I'm sorry." "Oh no worries, I'll try to remind you next time. You're doing great!"

At the end of the class, our instructors asked if we had any questions. Ever the teacher's pet, I raised my hand.

"How do you make the judgment of when to keep fighting versus when to run away?" I asked.

She instantly began explaining my legal rights. "If you seriously injure or even kill your attacker, you are not liable because it was done in self-defense . . ."

Only in a city as litigious as New York would they explain the liability of fighting off a mugger.

I should've been flattered, but the likelihood of my destroying my assailant too thoroughly was not my concern.

"I meant, more for my own safety."

"Oh." I could see her mentally readjust to the average-wimp mind-set. "Then you stop fighting when the other person is no longer a threat." She must have seen the disbelief on my face, because she then advocated a minimum of three months' instruction in order to master the basic skills.

I was intimidated but also inspired. Most of the advice for women on how to protect themselves focuses on preventing an attack. While this information is valuable, it teeters dangerously on victim-blaming, implying that women have control over every random criminal who might want to hurt us. I liked that this instructor could look me in my scared saucer eyes, and tell me that, with time, I had the ability not only to avoid an assault, but to stop one.

As my friend and I walked home, we each felt happy we'd taken the class, despite the unfortunate side effect of eyeing every man on the street with suspicion.

We both also agreed we'd take a full course of classes.

Because the only thing scarier than learning Krav Maga?

Not learning it.

Labor Day

. . . .

By Lisa

It was the summer of our discontent.

Where to begin?

An earthquake, a hurricane, and a visit from Mother Mary.

A disaster trifecta.

The perfect storm of catastrophes.

The Manny, Moe, and Jack of nightmares.

Just kidding.

She was here for two months, and now that she has gone back to Miami, I miss her. When I feel sad, I turn on *Everybody Loves Raymond,* really really REALLY LOUD.

And then I don't miss her anymore.

She came up because a sewer main broke under her house, necessitating all manner of repair work, and I figured it would be best if she weren't there to tell the workmen they were working too hard or they were really cute.

But we got off to a rocky start, which is to be expected, as we met only fifty-six years ago.

Here's our problem. We both have our own way of doing things. Actually, to be accurate, we have the exact same way of doing things, but we still disagree.

This is even harder than it sounds.

Spaghetti is a case in point.

I think it should be cooked for six minutes, or *al dente*. She thinks it should be cooked for thirty minutes, or *al dentures*.

That's Italian for mushy.

She thinks my spaghetti tastes like sticks, and I think hers doesn't taste.

Of course, we're both adamant about our cooking times. That's what I mean when I say we do things the same way. We're both adamant, all the time, about everything. Adamance runs like lifeblood in Scottoline women. If I die driving off a cliff, just know I was going the right way.

So at our first spaghetti meal, Mother Mary and I strike a compromise. I cook the spaghetti for eighteen minutes, which is too soft for me and too chewy for her.

The only thing we agree on is that we both hate compromise.

The next night, I try a different take.

Lying.

If you can't lie to you mother, who can you lie to?

So I tell her I cooked the spaghetti for thirty minutes even though I didn't, because she can't see the clock anyway.

Also, we disagree on whether to salt the water. I never salt it, but she always does. I think if we salt it, I'll get high blood pressure and die. She thinks if we don't salt it, we'll be defying centuries of Italian culinary history, so we might as well be dead.

Either way, spaghetti is life-or-death.

If you don't think your dinner is a medical emergency, you're not adamant enough.

It occurs to me, at one point, that we should try and negotiate, so I tell her I'll salt the water if she lets me cook the spaghetti for less time, but she won't go for it, and we have gridlock that even Congress can't match.

Because they're not adamant enough, either.

That's the problem with the Democrats and Republicans in Washington. They're just too flexible. Too willing to listen to

Mother Mary has to wait for her food to cook the way she likes it.

each other. To see the other side. To work together and cooperate, for the greater good.

Scottolines don't make fundamental mistakes like that.

We show no such lapses of judgment.

Those politicians should come over to my house and take a lesson. Mother Mary and I could school those pikers. They're adamance rookies. They might be able to shut down a government, but we can shut down a *kitchen*.

Which would you miss first?

I know.

So the solution for our spaghetti war was simple, and we did it the rest of the summer. I boiled two pots of pasta, each time. One was salted and one wasn't. One was cooked properly.

And one wasn't.

Thus we resolved our impasse. Or our impasta.

Sorry.

Of course, most nights, the temperature in the kitchen hovered at three hundred degrees.

But that had nothing to do with boiling water.

And we never got to eat at the same time, either. I ate during the first half of *Seinfeld,* and she ate during the second half, so it worked out fine, by Scottoline standards.

You can't have your spaghetti, and eat it, too.

I Stink, Officially

By Lisa

One of the good things that happened this summer was that I won an award, from a magazine that gives out Best of Philly awards.

I didn't win one of those.

I won Worst of Philly.

I hate to brag, but I won for Worst Columnist.

Yay! Thanks, magazine.

I was hoping it came with a car, or maybe some money, or a book entitled How Not to Suck.

But I'm not holding my breath. It's the thought that counts.

Why am I so happy?

I love having haters. It means I'm getting somewhere. Someone cares enough to hate me.

It used to bug me, but now I revel in it. This is the best attitude to have in my business, where you get your report cards from magazines, newspapers, and anybody with Internet access. I used to cry and worry, but now I just laugh. Unfortunately, Mother Mary doesn't feel the same way, and she was here when I won.

It wasn't pretty.

But it has a surprise ending.

I found out in the morning, when I got an email from a

beloved reader, who shows excellent taste in literature, except that she also reads this magazine. She wrote and told me that I had won the Worst Columnist award, and I laughed.

Mother Mary was next to me at the time, sitting at the kitchen island, having her mug of morning coffee. A whitish hunk of powdered sugar donut floated inside, like an iceberg with saturated fats. She asked, "What's so funny?"

"Nothing," I answered, wisely. I was lying to protect the magazine staffers. I know what she's capable of.

Vendetta is an Italian word, for a reason.

She may be eighty-seven, but she can still wield a wooden spoon.

And she has a history of defending me that would shame a grizzly. Once, when I worked in a law firm, and she thought I was working too hard, she told me she wanted to call the principal. In elementary school, when I got yelled at for something I didn't do, she wanted to call the governor.

Funny, the governor also won a Worst of Philly award, for Worst Sports Column, but I didn't tell my mother that, either.

Personally, I don't want my governor to be a good sports columnist.

"No, really, what's so funny?" Mother Mary asks. "What are you looking at on the computer?"

"Porn."

"That's not funny."

"I know, I'm the Worst Columnist. It says so, right here."

"*Who* says that?" Her cloudy brown eyes flare behind her trifocals. She has a temper that goes from zero to explosive in sixty seconds. Nitroglycerin has a higher flashpoint.

"A magazine says it."

"Where? I want to see it!" Her face flushes, and she becomes a human thermometer, with all the blood rushing to her bulb.

"I don't have the magazine to show you."

She waves me off, with an arthritic hand. "Oh, you're only kidding. They don't say it. You're gonna give me a heart attack."

"No, I'm not kidding. They really said it."

"Then prove it. Show me the magazine."

"But I'd have to go out and buy it, and I don't want to."

"GO BUY IT!" Mother Mary points to the front door, and her sugar donut sinks into her coffee. So I leave the house, get in the car, drive to the store, and buy the magazine that officially trashes me, in print.

I bring home the magazine and show it to her.

"I can't read this magazine! The print is too small!"

So I read it to her. "It says I'm the Worst Columnist, see? Here?"

Mother Mary peers at the paragraph, red-faced. "This is terrible!"

"Not really, Ma."

"Yes, it is! They didn't mention *me*!"

You're So Vain, This Is About You

....

By Francesca

Writing memoir can get complicated, especially when you write about love. Each time I refer to a guy I've dated, I agonize over what they'll think when they read it.

I'm a writer, but I'm still a person.

So I take great pains to disguise their identities. I consider it my duty to protect them this way—unlike fiction, I don't own their characters, and my perspective is a subjective one. By the time my story goes to print, their own mothers wouldn't recognize them.

But while they may be anonymous to other readers, it's possible that they could recognize themselves.

And that kept me up at night. Until I realized one important fact:

The men in my life don't read me.

Well, my father does, but that's what dads are for—making your boyfriends look inadequate.

I'm talking about the men I date. And I've dated wonderful, supportive, intelligent guys. They seem interested in a lot of things about me, except my job. I try not to let it bother me.

But it does.

One time, a reader wrote my mom, saying that she thought I would be a great match for her son. Her son was supersmart, very successful, and a bona fide nice guy, so my mom passed along my info. We ended up going out a handful of times, and by all accounts everything in the description was 100% true. But I did have a funny conversation with him:

"I have a confession to make," he said. "I've never read your column."

I was surprised. Not because I expect guys in their early thirties to be reading the column, but this was a blind date, a setup *based* on my easily-Google-able, 700-word column. What if he disagreed with his mother and thought I sounded awful? Wasn't he curious?

"Then what made you want to meet me?" I asked.

"I liked your picture."

There's a reason no one ever wrote a book called *The Masculine Mystique*.

But his apathy is not unique. Even boyfriends I've dated seriously, men I have loved, don't read my writing.

I wrote a short novel as my senior thesis in college, and in it, I gave the love interest the same name as my ex-boyfriend. The character wasn't based on him, but I found using his name in the first draft helped trigger some of the emotions I needed to express for the story. I always intended to change it. My ex went to my college, and I didn't think my new boyfriend, also a classmate, would appreciate the homage.

But then my thesis advisor thought the new name I suggested sounded too much like another character's, and somehow in the haste of editing on a deadline, it remained. My thesis went on to win an award, and as part of the honor, the university produced bound copies to be displayed on a front shelf in the library.

I should have been celebrating, but instead I felt sick. What would happen when they read it? I braced myself for the awkward conversations and hurt feelings sure to be coming my way. Any minute now.

Luckily I didn't hold my breath. Neither of them cracked the cover.

Maybe it's a gender thing. There are different expectations for men and women in relationships. In high school, even in the 2000's, I remember boys would ask their girlfriends to watch their sport's practice. As if watching a bunch of sweaty, pimply adolescent boys run drills could possibly be entertaining. But girls would do it!

Thank God my first boyfriend was a band geek, so I didn't have to endure this tedium.

See, I can call him that because he'll never know.

Women are trained to show interest in every aspect of men's lives, and men are trained to believe they are fascinating. Meanwhile, women are mocked in movies and sitcoms for wishing their boyfriends or husbands would ask about their day.

The nerve!

I'm not against supporting your partner, I'd just love to see some sixteen-year-old boys watching field hockey practice.

And it's not that I want my ex-boyfriends to be obsessed with me. On the contrary, I want them to move on (slowly), date other people (after I start seeing someone first), and be (almost as) happy (as I am).

Ex-boyfriends should have a greater stake in their former flames' creative output, because they might show up in it.

Think of Carly Simon's famous lyric, "You're so vain, you probably think this song is about you." For the last forty years, fans have tried to guess which famous ex-lover she's addressing. Is it Mick Jagger? Warren Beatty?

The mystery was fun, but it didn't really matter. What made the song awesome was the idea of an old boyfriend pining away, deluding himself that he still matters, while his ex, once jilted, now rocks out at his expense.

If living well is the best revenge, the second best is a hit record.

But last year, Simon released a new edition of the song, promising it would answer the riddle of the man's identity, and sure enough, if you play the song backwards, you can hear her whisper: "David."

David? Bowie? Cassidy?

David *Geffen,* according to *The Sun* and *Us Weekly.* Not an ex-lover at all, but the gay record executive who headed her then-label Elektra. Supposedly, Simon blamed Geffen for favoring rival singer Joni Mitchell over her.

Boring.

But typical. I'm sure Jagger and Beatty were vain, too, but they were probably also too self-absorbed to be poring over the lyrics to their old girlfriend's song.

Adele's infamous ex might be the only person on earth who hasn't heard her album.

If my ex-boyfriend wrote a hit album after we broke up, I would hold a stethoscope to the stereo speakers and replay it for a panel of my girlfriends.

In fact, my last boyfriend was a singer-songwriter, and although he had many delectable traits, this one excited me most. The way I saw it, it was win-win—whether our relationship became a true-love affair or a fiery train wreck, I could end up in a song!

One day, I asked him if he ever wrote songs about women from his past or present (wink wink, nudge nudge).

He said no, not really, he just made them up.

Even the girls' names in his songs?

Whatever rhymes.

A cleverly diplomatic answer, I thought, but I didn't believe it. Instead I cursed my mother for giving me such an un-rhymeable first name. I can't even work my name into a limerick:

There once was a girl named Francesca . . .

In the end, we split up amicably, I got no souvenir song, and my only parting gift was five breakup pounds.

Now if he read this, I would never cop to the weight gain. Luckily I don't have to worry.

So I'm still longing for the artist whom I can inspire or, at the very least, damage.

I'd love to be a masterpiece, but I'll settle for your severed ear.

I think most women find the notion of being a muse romantic. So why don't men?

Maybe it's because the role of the artist's muse was historically female, so men don't share the fantasy.

Well, that's not true either, because history has been rewritten as of late. Experts now believe that Shakespeare likely wrote his love sonnets about a young man, and Da Vinci's *Mona Lisa* was a portrait of his pretty-boy assistant.

Historical proof all the good ones are gay.

But these straight men are missing out. Guys, don't you see? This is your chance at real immortality—not with sperm but with ink. The pen is mightier than the penis! You can leave your mark on the world without having to pay for its college tuition.

Are you a great lover? Get it in writing!

Are you a total jerk? Revel in your infamy!

Or don't. I'm over it. I'm not writing to get male attention anyway. I write to share my perspective, laugh at myself, and hopefully connect to my lovely, intelligent, and sensitive readers. My boyfriends may not be among them, but that's for the best. It's better I be uninhibited, or at least it's more fun that way. Like my favorite Real Housewife and spiritual leader Camille Grammar says, freedom is a girl's best friend.

When I first tell guys I'm a writer, they'll often make a joke along the lines of, "Uh-oh, I better be good. I don't want to end up in a book!"

I always smile and assure them they have nothing to worry about.

And I mean it.

What they don't know won't hurt them.

Shortcut Sally

· · · · · · · · · · · · · · · ·

By Lisa

The world divides into two categories of people: Those Who Like Shortcuts, like me, and Those Who Don't, like Daughter Francesca.

These worlds collided last week, when I was in New York visiting her.

Before I explain, let me point out that I don't take shortcuts in everything. In fact, once again, the world divides into two categories: Things In Which I Never Take Shortcuts, like my writing, and Things In Which I Always Take Shortcuts.

Which is everything else.

Most of the time, this serves me well. For example, I couldn't figure out how to program my VCR, so I never did, and that didn't hurt me in the end, because now VCRs are extinct.

Joke's on you, VCRs.

To follow up, I got a DVD player, but I couldn't figure out how to attach it to my new big TV, so I didn't bother. And that didn't matter either, because my cable company invented On Demand.

Comcastic!

See, if you just wait long enough, some problems solve themselves, which is a special form of shortcut.

In fact, my favorite.

It works well, but don't try it at home if you're not an expert, like me. It requires years of practice ignoring things, and you have to know which things to ignore. I also have a genetic predisposition, as Mother Mary is a master at ignoring things, like oxygen and me.

I've been living my life, taking my shortcuts, but it became a problem visiting Francesca, because she doesn't. We were doing things around her apartment when we decided to hang up four pictures. They were of equal size, and they had to be mounted in a straight line. Francesca has her way to do it, and I have mine.

The shortcut!

I grab the hammer and want to bang a nail into the wall, hang the print, eyeball it, then hang the second print next to it. If it's not level, I'll take off the print, pull out the nail, and hammer in another nail. It won't matter, because all the nail holes will be hidden behind the picture and no one will ever know.

You may recall that I'm the girl who painted around my pictures rather than taking them down and painting the wall.

Francesca says, "We should measure before we hang them. Each print is six inches across, and if we leave two inches between each one, we can make a little tick mark on the wall and . . ."

I stop listening. I love her, but I hate math. Discussion ensues, after which I say, "Look, you wanna do it yourself?"

"Yes," Francesca answers, already reaching for the hammer, as she knows me and loves me anyway.

Ten minutes later, we have a second incident, when we were unpacking a new carbon-monoxide detector. By way of background, Francesca has a detector in the hallway of her apartment, and it had gone off in the middle of the night, as had her neighbor's. Her super had determined that the cause was a waning battery, and not lethal gas.

Good to know.

But being the excellent mother that I am, I wanted her to have an extra detector in her bedroom, so we bought one. It said on the package that all you had to do to install it was to plug it into an electrical socket, which is my kind of installation. If VCRs had worked that way, they'd still be around.

Let that be a warning, laptops.

Anyway, I'm about to plug the detector into a power strip when Francesca notices a little door on the back. "Look," she says, pointing. "It has a place to put in a battery, for backup."

I think, *So what?* I've never put in a backup battery in my life. I have plenty of appliances, from alarm clocks to coffeemakers, and they all have little doors for backup batteries, but I don't bother. People who love shortcuts scoff at backup batteries. And when I look at the little door on the detector, I notice that it requires a screwdriver to open.

I say, "Let's just plug it in. It's too much trouble to get the screwdriver."

"But what if it falls out of the surge protector? Doesn't that mean it won't work?"

I think, *Well, yes. Technically.*

Francesca shrugs. "It probably doesn't matter. Let's just plug it in."

But I look at her big blue eyes, and I love her more than shortcuts.

At least this particular shortcut.

"I'll go get the screwdriver," I tell her.

Doggie Universe

· · · · · · · · · · · · · · · ·

By Lisa

You would think that if you live alone, you get to be the boss.

As in, you're not the boss of me.

Because now that it's only me, I should be the boss of me.

In fact, I'm self-employed, so I am, literally, my own boss. But that's just literally, or maybe for tax purposes, but not in real life. In real life, my dogs are the boss of me.

And my cats are my slavemasters.

I realized this a moment ago, when I was working on my laptop, with two dogs sleeping on either side, Peach and Little Tony, each with its head on my lap. I like to work with the TV on, and some horrible show came on, but I couldn't reach the remote to change the channel without waking up Little Tony. And he's cranky when he wakes up. In fact, he growls if you move him once he's asleep.

He's not a morning dog.

So I let sleeping dogs lie, and it became the moment when I realized that I wasn't the boss of me. The only way it could have been clearer was if the show on TV was *Who's the Boss?*

Answer: Little Tony Danza.

Something similar had happened the night before, during which I slept with three dogs. Why three? Because two slept on the floor.

Even *they* didn't want to sleep with three dogs.

Normally I sleep with Peach and Little Tony, and they flank me at night, one on my left side and one on my right, their positions as established as seats at a family dinner table. We arrived at this arrangement because they're jealous of each other, and they fight at night.

Over me.

Yes, I still got it.

Peace is maintained if one dog sleeps on either side, with me in the middle, like a postmenopausal Switzerland.

But I'm dog-sitting for Daughter Francesca's Cavalier, named Pip, and it put us over the top. Who knew that Pip would be the tipping point?

Or the Pipping point?

We all went to bed last night, and Peach and Little Tony

Not only do the dogs take over, so does Mimi.

settled into their customary positions. Evidently this left Pip feeling as if he had nowhere to sleep, so he spent the night walking around the bed, trying to cuddle with my head, then moving down by my feet, then circling up to my head again, orbiting me until dawn. Of course, that created a disturbance in the canine solar system, roughly akin to the introduction of a new planet.

Do you want to tell Jupiter to move over?

I don't.

Especially not if Jupiter growls.

So Peach and Little Tony went into their own new orbits, and everybody circled me all night long, trying and rejecting their different sleeping spots, hoping to reconfigure their canine galaxy.

I was at the center, like a cranky sun.

Just because I'm postmenopausal doesn't mean I'm post-cranky.

I'm still a woman.

I think.

Anyway, I started to worry that all of this intergalactic travel would mean that Peach would need to go to the bathroom, which created its own problem. I was too tired to get up and take her out, but not tired enough to go back to sleep and just forget about it. In fact, I have been known to wake up at night and *not* go to the bathroom because I didn't want to wake Peach, because then I'd have to take her out.

In other words, Peach's bladder trumps mine.

And isn't that the way, with pets?

And owners like me?

I'm not a boss, I'm a people-pleaser.

And now I'm a pet-pleaser.

And I wouldn't have it any other way.

Unspecial Delivery

By Francesca

I recently moved to a new apartment, so now I get to start the happy business of furnishing it. Already, this is an easier process than it was in my old place. In my last apartment, the "living room" was like a bowling alley but not as long. It was so narrow, the heat from the TV screen could warm you on the couch—like a crackling fire with commercial breaks.

Although it was fun to realize my childhood fantasy of living like *The Boxcar Children,* it was an inconvenient layout for home furnishing. Thankfully, my new apartment has a more sensible layout and is sized for adult humans, so I've been saving up to get the coffee table of my dreams.

I found one I loved, but it was at the top of my price range. I needed a bargain, or better, I wanted a *steal.* So I staked out the company website, waiting for a sale. Every plan needs a man on the inside, so I went to the store a few times to befriend a salesperson—code name: Brendan, real name: also Brendan.

After months of lying in wait, a sale popped up.

I was on the phone with my boy that very day. I had just recited my credit-card number into the phone when Brendan said, "Now, as far as shipping, we recommend white-glove delivery with this item."

I asked how much that cost.

He told me and I almost dropped the phone.

I assured him "standard" was fine.

"Just to be clear, standard delivery means curbside."

Curbside? Even Domino's will bring the pizza to your door.

I live in New York City; anything left curbside will be either stolen or peed on by about fifty passing dogs and several humans.

"For ninety-nine dollars more, we also have the 'Room of Choice' delivery option."

I live in a tiny apartment, there's really only one room to choose.

And for ninety-nine dollars, they *still* won't open the package for me?

Brendan, I thought we were friends.

"The nice thing about white-glove delivery is that they'll make sure the item is not damaged in any way."

I said I assumed if the table came damaged, that wouldn't be my problem.

"But in that case, we can't know whether the item arrived damaged or if you damaged it."

Presuming the buyer is lying at all times—customer service for the new economy.

He continued, "With white-glove service, they'll unpack it, inspect it, assemble it, and clean up the mess." He proceeded to go into a lengthy explanation of how the glass is delivered in a wooden crate that's hard to dispose of, etc., etc.

I interrupted that, while I appreciate the heads-up, I don't need to pay someone to take out the trash.

"It's not just that. The glass top weighs about 150 pounds," he said. "It's difficult even for me. There's no way a woman could lift it."

I wondered if he could hear my jaw set.

I don't like to be told I can't do something. I get that from Mother Mary.

And I'm not some dainty little lady. I work out lifting weights. I can squat over 100 lbs. Admittedly, that requires me getting the thing across my back. Here, we're talking about a large, round, unwieldy piece of glass, and with Pip as my only spotter, it didn't sound like a wise move.

But the cost of white-glove delivery would cancel out any discount earned during the sale. I smelled a conspiracy.

But people who believe in conspiracies aren't taken seriously, so I couldn't say that. Instead, I thought of the one person who's always taken seriously.

Mom.

WWMD?

So in my best Mean Mommy tone, I told him I was "very disappointed" in these options and I would have to think about it.

Then I didn't call what'shisname back for two whole days.

On the third day, he called me saying they could add on an employee "Friends and Family" discount to my sale price.

They only want you when they can't have you.

Salesmen are still men.

We had a deal! Two weeks later, my long-awaited table was set to arrive. I could finally stop drinking my coffee out of an adult-size sippy cup.

I don't know what I expected "white-glove" deliverymen to look like, but the two cranky, schlubby guys frowning at me from my doorway were not it.

Is there some rule that deliverymen must be paired in the style of Mutt and Jeff? There's always a short, squat one and a tall, reedy one. Ironic in a profession that requires carrying things at more or less the same height.

And there's only ever one who does the talking, while the other stands mute. I'm always suspicious that the talker is keeping the tips to himself.

The two rushed in with the *cardboard* box (wooden crate, my foot) and assembled the table so quickly you'd think they were contestants on *Minute to Win It*.

They were almost out the door when I realized the table's asymmetrical legs did not match the picture on the instructions, and I called them back.

Jeff said they had built it correctly, the instructions were wrong.

Mutt blinked in agreement.

I wasn't buying it.

Well, technically I'd already bought it, but I wasn't happy. So we went back and forth about it, and in the end, Jeff won, because I couldn't figure out how to make it match the diagram either. I had to let them go.

After they left, I got the bright idea to make a paper-doll version of all the table's parts so I could experiment with the assembly.

So there I was, sitting on the floor with my arts and crafts project, rapidly cutting and folding like some master of origami, when—*Eureka!* In making my model, I had identified the mistake and knew how to fix it.

Guy Fieri, where's my million dollars?

With no time to lose, I bolted from my apartment, burst on to the street, and ran down the delivery truck just as it was rounding the corner. When the truck stopped to see what this madwoman was doing, I actually leapt up to the driver's side and stuck my head in the window.

"You have to come back," I panted. "I figured it out."

"We have other deliveries to make, and you already signed for it—"

If they didn't think I was crazy already, they knew for sure when I exploded with, "THIS IS WHITE-GLOVE DELIVERY!"

And back they came. I showed them my paper-crane model, and they begrudgingly reassembled it. I thanked them, they grunted and left.

When Brendan called to check how my delivery had gone, I told him the whole story. He seemed genuinely frustrated for me, which made us friends again.

"You're sure it's right now?" he asked.

I said yes.

"If there's any other problem, call me. I'll come to your apartment and fix it myself."

Now that's customer service.

There Was a Little Girl,
Who Had a Little Curl

● ● ● ● ● ● ● ● ● ● ● ● ● ● ● ● ● ●

By Lisa

I thought the days were over when I worried about my grades, but I've been checking the mail with college-acceptance levels of anticipation.

Let me explain.

A few years ago, I went to my great cardiologist for a checkup, and he did a blood test that showed my cholesterol was 258, which was high. Oddly, this was about the same as my math SAT score, which was lower than low. In fact, it was downright embarrassing and maybe half my brain is missing.

The cardiologist explained that cholesterol is composed of bad cholesterol, or LDL, and good cholesterol, or HDL. I remember which is which by thinking that the L stands for lousy and the H stands for you can buy green bananas.

Also I had something called triglycerides, but I didn't know what they were, only that I had 67 of them. I don't know how many biglycerides I had.

2?

So okay, in the olden days, my LDL was 149, which earned me a bold-faced **HIGH** on the results, though my HDL was also **HIGH**, at 96. Basically I had a whole lot of bad and a whole lot of good in me.

So when I'm good, I'm very, very good.

And when I'm bad, I divorce somebody.

You probably know what cholesterol is, but I read on the Internet that it's a waxy gook that creates plaque on the wall of your arteries. I always thought that a plaque on your wall was a good thing, but no.

Apparently, something had to be done about my cholesterol, and it didn't help that I had gained a little weight.

I was cholesteroly-poly.

So the cardiologist told me to exercise and put me on Crestor, and in no time, my grades improved. My cholesterol dropped to 164, and my LDL to 66, even though my HDL stayed **HIGH** at 88, but that was all good. I became an honors student, even though it took drugs, but that's okay. Half of the student population is on drugs, and at least mine were advertised on TV, albeit by men with gray hair.

My prostate's fine, thanks.

But a few months ago, I started to dislike the idea of being on a drug for the rest of my life. I began to take my award-winning cholesterol for granted. In other words, I was on a cholester-roll.

Sorry.

Also, Crestor cost a mind-blowing $400 a month, which my high-priced, top-drawer health insurance declined to cover. I pay for Personal Choice, but it turns out that the company is the one with the personal choice.

They chose not to cover me, but I didn't take it personally.

Because they don't cover anybody.

My cardiologist even appealed, but they turned us down, so every month, I had four hundred reasons why I hated being on Crestor.

On top of the many more reasons I have for hating my insurance company.

So I asked the cardiologist if I could go off the drug and see what happened. He said sure, give it a try for three months, and told me to make sure I ate the right foods, exercised, and kept my weight down. So I did, experimenting on myself, throughout the summer. I became my own guinea pig, without the piggy part.

I dieted, I worked out, and I hosted a visit by Mother Mary, which did wonders for my cholesterol because I forgot about it in favor of my blood pressure.

But two weeks ago, I took one last blood test and just got back my cholesterol scores. And they were as disappointing as my SAT scores. Nothing I did worked. My cholesterol is back up to 233, which earned me another bold-faced **HIGH**, and my LDL is also **HIGH** again, at 129.

So I'm back to being very, very good and very, very bad again, and you know what that means.

I should divorce my insurance company.

Final Curtain

· · · · · · · · · · · · · · · · ·

By Lisa

More misadventures in home makeover, this time with curtains.

I recently painted my family room myself, on a Type A tear, but I took the Scottoline route. By which I mean, I took shortcuts. Lots of them.

I painted around pictures rather than removing them, and the paint only reached five feet six inches up the wall, which is my height plus my arm length, minus a ladder, which I don't own.

This would be the mathematical formula for do-it-yourself wainscoting.

You could barely tell since I used the same color, which was white, but about two years later, I started hating that my walls were white. So I went crazy and hired real painters to make the family room a gorgeous yellow. And it looks so yummy, like melting butter on a stack of pancakes.

If your walls look fattening, you picked the right color.

But then I started to notice that I had no curtains in the family room.

Correction.

I have no curtains anywhere in the house. All my windows are bare. Sometimes this bothers me, like when I'm bare.

But mostly I stay away from the windows at times like that,

and there are only trees around me anyway. Still it's a little creepy late at night, when I'm working in the family room and those scary commercials come on for *Saw 5* and *Hostel 6*.

I'm hostile to *Hostel* movies.

I hate movies where people get murdered, especially when they distract me from writing novels where people get murdered.

Anyway, since I was worrying about psycho killers and also classing up my house in general, I thought I'd get some curtains on my windows, but I didn't know where to buy some. I asked Best Friend Franca, and she knew somebody who made them, and long story short, the curtain lady came over and showed me a yellow swatch, which was perfect, with cottony white flowers on a buttery yellow background. A few months later, the curtains were ready, and the lady came and put them up. I stood, watching in happy amazement. They looked beautiful.

It wasn't until the next day that I saw the problem.

They were covered with black flecks.

I didn't see them from a distance, but close up, they were obvious. It looked like mold, and I panicked, running to check the furniture, to see how I had grown mold overnight.

But I hadn't.

The only moldy things were the curtains.

So I emailed the curtain lady, who called the manufacturer, and they said that the curtain material was supposed to be that way. The black flecks weren't mold, but authentic bits of cotton seed, which was supposed to be in the fabric.

This would be the proverbial good and bad news: Your new curtains aren't moldy, they just look that way.

My curtains have fake mold. Or in decorating terms, faux mold.

I tried to visualize the flecks as something other than mold, but it didn't help. They also looked like dirt, but I'd like to dirty my curtains myself, not have them come pre-filthy. The flecks also look like black pepper, but I can't remember the last time I seasoned a fabric.

It gives new meaning to a high-fiber diet.

Meanwhile, I own a lot of cotton clothing, and none of it retains its cotton seeds. This would be like lumber that comes with its own family of squirrels.

I went and checked my sample swatch, and it has no fake mold.

In fact, I held the swatch up to the curtains, and they were so different, it looked like the Before and After pictures in a Proactive commercial.

My curtains have blackheads.

Then I realized what had happened. The swatch is only three inches by three inches, and if I looked hard enough on the curtains, I could find maybe one or two three-inch patches without the black dots, but they were the rare exception, not the rule.

Bottom line, I'm calling the manufacturer.

It's a clear case of bait and swatch.

Emotional Baggage

· · · · · · · · · · · · · · · ·

By Francesca

Old habits die hard.

I was reminded of this many times during my mom's last visit to New York. I had just moved into a new apartment, and my mom wanted to stay and help me set up my new place. In the process, she noticed my old television was gone; in fact, it had short-circuited and had to be thrown out.

"I still can't believe that TV broke already," she said. "That was a new TV."

"We got it my freshman year of college."

"Exactly."

"Mom," I said. "That was seven years ago."

She looked stunned.

Listen, I don't like to face it any more than she does.

She asked, "You couldn't get a TV repairman to look at it?"

"I don't think they exist anymore. Anyway, it'd be cheaper to buy a new one."

My mom shook her head. "I sound like Mother Mary, don't I?"

I laughed. "Kinda."

We unpacked all day and ordered health-food takeout for dinner. After fifteen years living in a place so remote they can't deliver a pizza, my mother thinks takeout-anything is paradise.

"So we'll have to get up early tomorrow morning to buy a new TV," my mom said.

"In this city, the Best Buy is open twenty-four hours."

Her eyes lit up. "You mean, we could see that new Sarah Jessica Parker movie tonight, *then* go?"

"Why not?"

We were getting crazy now!

With our new devil-may-care attitude, we grabbed our things and hustled to the door. But mothers can only suspend their practicality for so long. She said, "Wait, you need a coat."

"I have a cardigan."

"It won't be enough, you'll be cold."

Did I mention it was August?

But that doesn't deter my mom. She said, "You'll freeze in the air-conditioning."

We went back and forth about it. I know my mom only wants to take care of me like she always has, but I'm twenty-five years old.

"I don't want to carry a coat around!" I stamped my foot.

Like I said, twenty-five years old.

"Fine. Then let me carry it for you. It'll make me feel better, okay?"

I couldn't argue with that. If she wanted to act like my foot-man, I figured I'd be a jerk not to let her. I gave in.

It was almost midnight by the time the movie had ended and we made it to Best Buy, my mother still schlepping the coat. The odd hour made the errand fun, the way being in school after hours felt reckless and exciting. But walking home with a brand-new TV in the city at midnight was crazy even for us, so I flagged down a cab to take us home.

"Look at you, honey, hailing a cab like a real New Yorker!" my mom said.

I love that my mom is easy to impress.

After a short ride, we were back on the curb in front of my building, with me holding the TV box and my mom holding . . .

Nothing.

We looked at each other, then down the street, where we watched the cab turn the corner and disappear from view, with my coat inside.

My mom turned back at me with a look of such cowering dread, like Kermit the Frog before a slap from Miss Piggy.

I was surprised, what did she think I was going to do?

Then I realized I was looking at the effects of PTTD—Post Traumatic Teenager Disorder.

She thought I was going to give her a hard time, like I might have done when I was young and obnoxious. But I've grown up since then, and I wasn't angry at all.

"Aw, Mom, don't feel bad. It's not your fault, I forgot about it, too."

"But I was supposed to hold it for you!"

"It was an accident, I leave things in cabs all the time, it's so easy to do."

"You didn't want to bring it!"

"You just wanted me to be comfortable, it was nice of you."

"No, you're the nice one. You're the best daughter."

"Aw, I love you."

"I love you too!"

We dissolved in a flurry of hugs and girl noises, my mom practically crying, my doorman rolling his eyes.

Five minutes later, we were still hugging and telling each other how great we were, when a car honked.

It was our cabbie, who had reappeared and was waving to us from his window.

"Lady, you forgot this?" he called, holding up the coat.

This was a New York miracle.

We ran over, thanking him profusely. He was very sweet, trying to refuse my mom's extra tip and our calling him a hero. We hugged him through the window, we were so happy.

The new couple in the backseat were less thrilled.

That night, I felt as if the universe was rewarding our new mature relationship, and the good karma of forgiveness brought the lost coat back to us.

Every mother-daughter relationship is a work in progress. I'm learning not to play the blame game, and my mom is learning that I can dress myself. Sometimes we'll get it wrong, sometimes we'll get it right. And we'll bore the tears out of every doorman in New York City.

Old times were great, but the new era looks better than ever.

Willpower and Won'tpower

· · · · · · · · · · · · · · · · ·

By Lisa

Now I've seen everything.

Apparently there are people in this world who are supposed to be working on their computers, but spend so much time cruising the Internet, playing online games, and posting on Facebook that they go out and buy an application to lock them out of their fun and games, so that they force themselves to use their computer only for work and research.

I'm not making that up.

The app is called Self-Control, and I'm not making that up, either.

Once you install Self-Control, it can't be disabled in any way, even by turning off the computer and restarting it. You install the app and set it for a certain amount of time, like three hours, and you get no access to any of your time wasters until the time is up.

Amazing, right?

And who are those people, who lack self-control to such an extent that they have to buy it?

Well, for starters, me.

In other words, if you lack maturity, there's an app for that.

I love this idea.

I haven't bought the Self-Control app, but I'm thinking about it, then I'm going shopping for all the other apps I need. Namely:

Eat too much chocolate cake?

There's an app for that.

Watch too much TV?

There's an app for that.

Yap on the cell phone until it singes your cheek?

There's an app for that, too.

With these apps, you can willingly give up your power to something that prevents you from having any fun at all.

Sounds like my second marriage.

Or, as I now think of it, my Thing Two app.

What a concept! An app is a chastity belt, for your life.

Here we are, living in the United States, a country that fought wars for its freedoms, and somehow we've come to the point where we have to pay a computer to take our freedoms away.

Because a machine has more common sense than we do. Though we, allegedly, have the brain.

Like the song says, lack of freedom isn't free.

Tell you what worries me about this.

Watson.

You know who that is, right? Watson is the computer who beat all comers at *Jeopardy!* Did you watch that? I did, with a sinking heart. The studio audience was all happy, full of shills for the IBM engineers who built Watson, but I feared for all of humankind.

Why?

Simple.

How are we going to win anything if the computers start going on game shows?

Mark my words. The cursor is on the wall, people.

The smartphones are already smarter than we are, and now the computers will be raking in all the cruises and refrigerators.

You can kiss that dinette good-bye, bucko.

The price may be right, but you aren't, when you play against your laptop.

And it gets worse.

I heard about an app that you install in your laptop, then you put your laptop between your mattress and box spring, and the app records your movements during the night. If you set the app's timer to wake you up within a half-hour period, it will wake you up when you're moving around the most. Theoretically, this would be when you weren't in your deepest sleep, and you'd wake up refreshed.

Okay, that's officially scary.

I want my computer asleep when I am.

I don't want my computer to know more about me than I do. The next thing you know, it'll be sneaking around my bedroom, trying on my jewelry and sticking its fingers in my face cream. My laptop has its own sleep cycle, and it should stay out of mine.

And what happens if you're the kind of person who sleeps with four dogs, all of whom walk around the bed all night, scratching, snorting, and farting?

I mean, who are these people who sleep with four dogs? And sometimes a cat?

Okay, that would be me, too.

That would create havoc with the app, if it was to measure the movement in my bed, which turned out to be Peach and Little Tony.

But enough about the movement in my bed.

In fact, there's not enough movement in my bed, of late.

Think there's an app for that?

Hairy and Crazy

· · · · · · · · · · · · · · · ·

By Lisa

It's that time of year, when spiders beat a path to my door.

I know.

Still got it.

As soon as I open my front door, big wolf spiders come from God-knows-where to run inside my house.

Of course I can't bring myself to kill them. Spiders are good bugs, even if they're scary and creepy, so I turn a glass upside down over them, slide a paper underneath, then flip the entire assembly right side up and throw the spider back outside.

But lately, I'm finding problems with my method.

First, it means that I always answer the door with a glass in my hand, like a drunk. The neighbors and the UPS guys are starting to look at me funny. I tell them it's because of the spiders, but the spiders hide when other people come over.

My UPS guy winks. "Right, the spiders. Gotcha."

It doesn't help that I usually come off slightly potted around this time of year, writing all day in sweatpants and frowzy hair, with my glasses cockeyed. It's not a good look for a single woman, and about the only thing it attracts is spiders.

Second, the spiders are onto me, and they think it's a game. This morning when I opened the door to get the newspaper, I had to throw out a huge wolf spider, and just now, when I went to take the dogs for a walk, the same spider tried to get back in.

And he was smiling.

He was so big that between the spider going in and the dogs and I going out, it was a traffic jam of furry legs.

Mine included.

The furriest.

Hey, it's fall, and that's how you know. My leg hair grows in, long and fluffy.

That's what women really mean when we say that we love the seasons. Half the year, we're not shaving our legs.

Men would never know, if I weren't busting us. They're too busy looking at our busts.

Which are unhairy, generally.

Or maybe that's another column.

To write when I'm drunk.

Or you are.

Anyway, the third problem with my method is that spiders network better than teenagers. They used to run in one at a time, but now each one is coming back with five hundred friends, and I bet they're all on Facebook and Twitter, calling for a flash mob at my doorstep.

They're LOL. And I'm WTF?

When four or five run at me, there aren't enough glasses to catch them all, and at the end of the day, I have a dishwasher full of glasses used only by spiders.

Half the time, there are no glasses left for my margarita.

Er, I mean, Diet Coke.

Plus, I don't have time to clean up after insects. Who needs it? I live alone. I'm an empty spider-nester.

I decided to use only the tallest glasses for spiders, but Daughter Francesca didn't know that, and the last time she visited, I caught her drinking out of one. I yelped, "Eeek, a spider glass!"

And she dropped it.

It must be a buggy time of year, because I just read in the newspaper that parts of the southeastern United States are being invaded by hairy crazy ants. I'm not making this up, and that's what they're called.

They don't shave in fall or winter, either.

They're called hairy because their abdomens are furry, unlike normal ants, and they're called crazy because they run superfast, in random directions. They swarm into homes and factories, trying to find warm places to live.

Eew.

And if a hairy crazy ant gets killed, it releases a chemical that cues the rest of the hairy crazy colony to attack. According to one entomology professor, "The other ants rush in. Before long, you have a ball of ants."

So I'm feeling lucky. My spiders run in a straight line, and I'm hairier and crazier than they are.

But I swear, the day I open my front door and a ball of spiders rolls toward me, I'm going out drinking.

With my UPS guy.

Very Personal Shopper

. . . .

By Lisa

It's the time of year when a girl's thoughts turn to fleece, and I buy a new pair of sweatpants.

Turned on yet?

You will be, at least if you're like me, a sweatpants fetishist.

Because these are great sweatpants.

I'm picky about sweatpants because I work at home, and so I live in them, especially when it gets cold outside. And after much trial and error, I've found the perfect pair, and I get new ones every few years, from the same website.

I went online just now to order a pair, but the website had changed, and I couldn't find my go-to sweatpants.

I didn't know where to go to.

The website takes literally the sports part of sportswear, categorizing its women's clothes by sport, such as Alpine Climbing, Skiing, Snowboarding, Biking, Rock Climbing, and Casual.

Of course I clicked Casual. It defines me to a T, and I already have all the Alpine Climbing and Snowboarding clothes I need.

Which is none.

So I was lost in the website, until Patrick found me.

Who's Patrick? I don't know, but all of a sudden, while I was clicking around, onto my laptop screen popped a little window, with a message:

Hi, this is Patrick. How can I help you?

I didn't understand. I never had this happen. I knew generally that you could chat online with a salesperson, but I didn't know they could appear out of nowhere, unbidden.

And I wasn't sure I liked the idea.

I thought what I was doing online was private.

But it isn't.

By the way, just to clarify, I'm never doing anything embarrassing online, except buying clothes with an elastic waistband.

But that's embarrassing enough.

Actually, I've been known to search Google for Elastic Waistband, and if you're doing that, you know you're single forever.

I don't understand how Patrick knew I was on the site. I've heard of a personal shopper, but this would be an example of a too-personal shopper.

Still I figured I'd answer Patrick, since I didn't want to waste more time, so I typed in the little window: **I'm looking for black sweatpants.**

Then I hit SEND, and a nanosecond later, Patrick wrote:

Hey there! Let me get you some ideas!

I didn't need any ideas, I needed my go-to sweatpants. Still I liked his can-do attitude and his exclamation points, so I waited.

Patrick wrote: **Click here for our tights for women!**

I groaned. I wasn't looking for tights. Guaranteed that someone whose sport is Casual doesn't need tights.

Plus, tights are not sweatpants. They're tight, which is why they call them tights, and that disqualifies them altogether, as far as I'm concerned. I never want to wear something Tight. The only thing worse would be something On Fire.

Yet I refrained from telling this to Patrick, and instead I wrote: **I don't really want tights. I want stretch sweatpants with an elastic waistband.**

He didn't write back for a moment, and I imagined that he

stepped away to vomit, or to tell the gang that Scottoline was online.

Then he wrote back: **You are probably looking for the Serenity Tights! Click here!**

I clicked away, and of course they weren't what I wanted. They were stretch tights for a yoga-thin twenty-five-year old, and I'm a middle-aged woman with high cholesterol.

In other words, I'm not serene.

I'm casual, but that's not the same thing.

I typed: **Thx, but what I'm looking for aren't tights. They're pants but not for outdoors.**

Patrick wrote back: **Yep, if you check the link, you will see that many of our tights are not formfitting and look like pants.**

So there I was, having a fight with a man I don't know and have never met. This would be a first. Usually men have to marry me before the fighting starts, or at least meet me.

But maybe I'm improving.

Then I remembered something, so I wrote: **I think they're called R5 sweatpants.**

And Patrick wrote back: **Thanks for that! Click here for the R1 pants!**

Aha!

I clicked, and they were the right ones, so our story has a happy ending.

Except that I'd remembered it wrong. R5 is my train, not my sweatpants.

But Patrick knew all that, I'm sure.

9/11, Ten Years Later

· · · · · · · · · · · · · · · · · · ·

By Francesca

I find myself standing within a tower of light. I am in the center of a square of forty-four giant searchlights, each one wide as a timpani drum, beaming heavenward. Across from me is a second, identical tower. A soft rain sparkles in the upper heights of the light shaft, but as the raindrops near the enormous lamps, the water evaporates, and clouds of steam billow back up into the sky like ghosts.

It's the tenth anniversary of September Eleventh, and this is the Tribute in Light.

Three years ago, when I first moved to New York City, I'd never have gotten this close to a 9/11 memorial. I wouldn't have felt right. I lived around the corner from a makeshift shrine called "Tiles for America," which covers a chain-link fence with commemorative tiles painted by children from around the world. Tourists come by and take pictures of it. I have never taken a picture of it. I sneak glances when I'm walking by with my dog, but it's not on our usual route.

Sometimes tourists asked me for directions to Ground Zero, I could tell them only that it's downtown. I had never been myself.

Although avoiding the site wasn't a deliberate decision, I can't say it was entirely an accident. I love this city, but I never feel like a "New Yorker" until I'm outside of it. In Philly, I'm a New Yorker, but in New York, I'm a Philadelphian. My experience of 9/11 is a part of that barrier. I watched the attacks from afar, safe in my suburban cocoon, where such horror seemed so unreal we first thought it was a hoax. Real New Yorkers witnessed the terror and the tragedy firsthand; their loss was personal and profound. I didn't feel entitled to their grief.

And so I didn't feel entitled to go to that hallowed ground as an outsider. I was afraid of seeming like an emotional tourist, marveling at a tragedy the same way one would marvel at any landmark. I didn't know how to express my grief without cheapening theirs.

On the tenth anniversary, however, things felt different. This year, I wanted to pay my respects. I just wasn't sure how.

A college friend of mine moved here from San Francisco, and now she's a member of a city choir. Her group was singing in a 9/11 memorial concert in a church uptown the day before the anniversary. I'd been meaning to see her perform for a while, and this seemed like a good time to start. I felt a little anxious when I couldn't get someone to go with me, but I had made up my mind.

I hailed a cab and gave the address of the church. The driver responded with the typical wordless nod and I climbed in. But once we were driving, he asked me why I was going to church on a Saturday afternoon. I told him.

"Very sad weekend," he said, making eye contact in the rearview mirror.

"It is," I said, shifting my gaze to the window. Then I started talking about choirs instead.

I arrived at the church early, but I like to be early when I'm nervous. The few people who were there were couples and families, and I felt conspicuously alone. I chose a spot halfway back at the far edge of the pew, which would be good in case I had to leave early. Not that I had plans afterwards.

Another person entered alone, an older woman dressed all in black, black sweater, black skirt, even black gloves.

She must have lost someone in the attacks, I thought. I wondered if it was her son or daughter, or maybe her husband. This is probably her regular church. She belonged here.

I questioned if I had the same right to this grief as she does. Is grief a right? A burden? A privilege? What do I owe this woman and these victims, if I can do anything at all?

The concert began. They sang a beautiful program of many different types of songs. One of the most moving pieces based its lyrics on a real soldier's last letter home before he was killed in Iraq. Listening to the music, I relaxed and felt my eyes wet.

I looked back at the woman in black. I saw she held a white tissue in her hand.

I stopped crying.

By the end, I was glad I had gone to the concert. But I went straight home afterwards.

The next day was Sunday, September 11. Like many, I watched the official World Trade Center site memorial service, where members of the victims' families read each name. I sat glued to the television. If I so much as stepped away to get a glass of water, I rewound the coverage to see those I had missed. Toward the end, I started to cry.

In the privacy of my apartment, I let myself feel that sorrow. I didn't know anyone who died in the attacks, but I know people like them. I have a friend who is twenty-five and working his first big job in finance, I have a father who goes to a tall, shiny office building every morning, and I have a mother who means the world to me.

I know the pain these victims' families feel, because I know

Tribute in Light, September 11, 2011

the love they have for those who passed. And although I cannot claim to know their personal loss, I can share in their grief.

Loss cannot be shared, but grief can.

So when my friend Courtney invited me to see the Tribute in Light with her later that evening, I wanted to go.

Courtney is one of my dearest friends from home, we've known each other since sixth grade. Today, she works for the architectural lighting firm that designed and constructed this memorial light installation. Its twin pillars of light echo the footprint of the Twin Towers, they reach four miles into the sky and are visible from sixty miles away. Courtney had spent every night last week standing at different points in Manhattan and New Jersey with a walkie-talkie, helping to make sure each of the eighty-eight 7,000-watt lightbulbs was perfectly aligned for the tenth anniversary of September Eleventh.

In fact, I was with Courtney ten years ago, when the attacks first happened. I was sitting behind her in our tenth-grade chemistry class when a teacher rushed in and turned on the TV above the blackboard. I remember Courtney's head tilted back and her shiny black ponytail touched my desk. Her pretty hair on my notepad was the last ordinary thing I saw that day. By the time my eyes followed hers to the television, the world had changed.

Now ten years later, I stand beside her at the foot of a memorial she helped create. I knew then that I could write about it. Even two kids from Pennsylvania, like my friend from San Francisco in the choir, could participate in this memory. We are a part of this now. We are a part of its light, and its voice, and its song.

That's the thing about grief; it makes room—the room to be close to someone you've never met, and to mourn someone you never knew. Grief is a conduit—for love, for compassion, for healing, and for grace.

Time has not diminished the loss. We will never forget. But more will come to remember. Our collective memory burns brighter than ever before, and so united, we can send the rain back up in light.

Gateway Paint

. . . .

By Lisa

I've become a pot addict.

No, not *that* kind of pot. I've never even tried that kind of pot. I stay away from all drugs except Crestor, which shows you the kind of party I am.

But now, I'm addicted to sample pots of paint.

No joke. I can't quit, and it all started so innocently.

With gateway enamel.

Here's what happened. I had just finished writing my next book, and if you're a loyal reader, you know that as soon as I type The End, I have to begin something. And not something that's work, but something that's fun, like painting the family room.

A freshly painted family room is fun for middle-aged women. In fact, a freshly painted family room is orgasmic for middle-aged women.

At my age, sex involves latex. And not *that* kind of latex.

Anyway, after my last book, I painted the family room and I did it myself. But this time, I had started thinking that my office needed to be repainted, but I wanted it done right this time, which meant by somebody who paints underneath the pictures on the wall.

In other words, not me.

I also wanted to pick the right color, and I've learned from my painting mistakes. If you recall, the shutters on the house were painted yellow, which I hoped would be sunshiny, but turned out bright enough to be a source of solar energy. And it was too expensive a mistake to correct, so I had to live with it.

I've made other expensive mistakes, notably Thing Two, but luckily, I didn't have to live with that one. Divorce is like remodeling your life. It's not a failure, it's a home improvement.

If you can change your family room, you can change your family.

I saw an ad for some high-end paint, and I liked the colors, but since it was expensive, I went online and ordered three sample pots, which is very unusual for me. I think the world divides into test-patch people and the rest of us. By this I mean, do you know those laundry bleaches, skin creams, hair dyes, and other scary things that tell you to test it on a patch of shirt, arm, or hair first?

Well, I never listen.

I go whole hog, right from the outset. I'm all in, from the jump. I say go for it and let the chips fall, which may be related to the divorce part, but let's not tarry, I'm trying to change my ways. So I got the sample pots and started sampling.

I was pretty sure one of the blue shades should work, but when I got them on my office wall, they were too restful. If I rest in my office, I can't afford to buy pretentious paint.

So the sample pots did their job, but I had three blue stripes on my office wall, which committed me to painting it, for sure. And by the way, I got a little crazy and painted some sample stripes on the second-floor hallway, so now I was committed to that, too. I went back online and ordered four more sample pots of a tasteful tan, then painted four more stripes, but again no dice. They were all too flesh-colored, and they looked like skin walls, which would be fine in Stephen King's office, but not mine.

Still, I was having a blast. It was a rush to paint outside the lines, and the stripes morphed into blocks, blotches, then swirls. I understood the rush that an artist might get, even though I was just a lady in the suburbs, vandalizing my own hallway.

I went back online again and ordered three pots of reddish shades, but they were too bright, then I ordered two more greenish shades, but they clashed with the rug, then I went for two more pinkish pots, and before I knew it, I had become a sample-pot addict.

Now, my second floor looks like a demented rainbow, I've spent too much money, and am no closer to choosing an office color. In fact, I forget the name of the color I almost like, because I didn't write down its name next to the sample blotch.

And I keep dreaming of ordering another few sample pots, of the lavender colors.

One is too many, and a thousand not enough.

Gateway Brownie

· · · · · · · · · · · · · · · · · ·

By Francesca

Drug memoir is popular these days, and I'm hopping on the bandwagon. James Frey may lie about his experiences to sound more extreme, but not me. My drug experience was so disproportionately horrible, it needs no embellishment.

I hit rock bottom with a brownie.

Like any good episode of *Intervention,* let me begin at the beginning.

I have never smoked anything in my life. Tobacco products hold zero appeal. I've seen cigarettes' effects on my grandmother's health, and I'll never forgive them.

In high school, I was kept happily busy with schoolwork, sports, and singing, and drugs scared the hell out of me. In tenth grade, I sucked helium at a girl's birthday party, and I was so paranoid about losing brain cells before the PSAT, I spilled a tearful confession to my mom the very next day.

Yes, I was a nerd.

In college, I was no longer afraid, but I remained uninterested. The potheads were entertaining only to other potheads. And while I had some vague awareness of cocaine use at parties, it was always taking place behind a bathroom door when I really had to pee.

Really girls, the ladies'-room line is long enough.

So at twenty-five years old, I had never tried a single puff of weed. I admit, sometimes I felt like I'd missed out on something. There was a whole swath of cannabis-related pop culture that went over my head. "Puff" was just a magical dragon, "Cheech and Chong" just sounds offensive. Blunt means lacking in tact. I love Bob Marley because he was a musical genius.

At least I'd always have something to lord over my future children.

Do as I say, and as I do.

And I could run for president.

I did not inhale, nor did I have sex with that woman.

But despite the occasional law abider's remorse, trying marijuana was not on my agenda. After college, you're really getting too old for it anyway. Remember that one friend in grade school whose parents were hippies—were they cool? No, they were unwashed and embarrassing. That's why your friend always wanted to sleep over at your house.

But all that changed last winter.

After a month of constant working and living like a hermit, I had just turned in our third book to the publisher. The Eagles were set to play for the NFC Championship, so I had invited my best friend, my guy friend, and his girlfriend over for a playoffs party. Before they came over, I cleaned my entire apartment, ordered two pizzas, and got all the ingredients to make Eagles-green margaritas.

My three friends arrived at my place from an earlier game-day get-together a little gigglier than usual, but nothing that couldn't be caused by a beer or two. So when my best friend produced a tinfoil-wrapped brownie from the last party, my only thought was:

Yay brownie!

"It's a pot brownie," the other said, sniggering.

"Oh." I was genuinely disappointed. I imagined it would

taste earthy and gross. Frankly, if it's not going to taste sweet, it's not worth the carbs. "No thanks."

"Try it, they're awesome. We each had like two at the party."

"And you feel okay?" I asked.

The consensus was that they hardly felt it at all. I believed them, a) because they weren't acting unusual, and b) because I had always guessed that hash brownies were something of an urban myth. It seemed like the Ouija Board of drug experiences, where you stir some herbal into your Betty Crocker mix and delude yourself into believing you can "feel it." Baking takes precision; I didn't think a stoner could pull it off.

Still, I wasn't that into the idea of eating the brownie. I'd come this far without trying any drug, why start now? And soon, the pizza arrived, which they ate ravenously, and I hoped we could forget it.

But my friends would not let it go. I could barely focus on watching the game for all their teasing. They thought I was being weird, boring, annoying, and paranoid to refuse a delicious and harmless pot brownie. We went back and forth about it for nearly forty-five minutes.

"Fine!" I snapped. "I'll eat the darn thing." I took a careful bite.

It was surprisingly good. It tasted exactly like a normal brownie, which triggered the sugar addict in me, and I gobbled it up.

I was literally dabbing the crumbs from my mouth when my best friend sat back on the couch, her affect sour.

"I don't feel so good," she said.

"Me neither," said my guy friend.

"Yeah, I've actually been feeling pretty nauseous for a while," said the third. "I don't know why anyone does this for fun."

I thought they were kidding. "Ha, ha, very funny."

The three of them sat silently on my couch, looking green.

"You cannot be serious," I said. "You *just* convinced me to eat this!"

But they were all too baked to appreciate the irony or my indignation. Somehow, the very moment that I succumbed to their peer pressure was the same instant the high hit them, hard. Suddenly the mood was serious and they were all professing their queasiness. My friend's girlfriend started freaking out, insisting she had "overdosed on marijuana." I told her there was no such thing, but she demanded I Google it or call the police.

I can only imagine the humiliation of calling the NYPD to tell them you feel sick from a pot brownie. I opted for "Google it."

But in the time it took me to locate online reassurance, there was a new demand being made.

"Change the channel, I need to watch something with a narrative!" she cried.

No one overreacts quite like an overeducated nerd.

"But, the game," I pleaded.

But these pastry junkies were not having it. You don't mess with someone tripping on refined carbohydrates. They wanted a movie and they wanted it now. Then they wanted glasses of water, which I fetched for them, and then blankets.

When one of them asked for a wastebasket, I knew I was in trouble.

Suddenly, it was surround-sound puking.

My one friend hurling in the trash can, my guy friend ralphing in my sink, and my best friend bolting for the bathroom. She didn't make it.

Remember that pizza I ordered?

My pristine apartment was now painted with it.

The worst part was, I sensed this Barfapalooza was just a sneak preview of my own impending doom. I didn't know how much sober-ish time I had left, so I fought my own impending high to clean up as much as I could. With leaden limbs and unrelenting seasickness, I felt like housekeeping on an Italian cruise ship.

No one was going home that night, so my next step was getting these tweakers to bed, but moving them anywhere was easier said than done. My guy friend is over six feet and 200 lbs, so when he decided to cuddle up on the dog bed, Pip and I had no choice but to let him. And my best friend was so off-balance, she was crawling around on the floor like an extra in *Saving Private Ryan.*

Somehow everyone found a place to lie down and sleep it off. The next morning, despite brutal headaches, we were grateful for our second chance. We had survived the world's lamest drug episode.

Not one of us had a single positive effect from that abominable baked good—baked *evil*, more like it. It was harrowing and yet, humiliating. I always thought the upshot of a bad choice was a good story, but this was just embarrassing.

I mean, a brownie? Really?

I suppose the lesson was this: If you're a square, embrace your squareness. Do a square dance. You have all the right angles. You're well balanced. Great things come in square packages.

Just say no to bake sales.

Bittersweet

• • • • • • • • • • • • • • • •

By Lisa

This Thanksgiving will be wonderful in some ways, and sad in others. In a holiday that's all about food, this one will taste bittersweet.

Because we just lost our friend and neighbor Harry. He passed away the other day at age ninety, in his home, next door.

I was out of town when it happened, though when I came back, I noticed that his light wasn't on at night, usually a warm yellow glow through the dark branches of the trees, jagged and bare now, like black lightning.

I suppose I should have realized he had passed, but I didn't, which is the paradox of death. It always comes as a surprise, even when it's expected. The shock arises from its very gravity.

I felt that way about my father's passing, ten years ago. I knew and I didn't know, both at once. I was completely prepared, and I wasn't prepared at all.

I still feel that way.

Harry didn't look well at his last birthday, when Francesca and I went over, bringing him a gift sweater we knew he'd never wear, because he loved his old cardigan. It was only a few months ago, but his sharp blue eyes had lost a little focus, as if his brain had loosened the reins. He was using a walker for the first time, this man who used to stride two miles around the block at a clip, tall and upright, waving a handkerchief at passing cars—as a warning, not a surrender.

Never a surrender.

Harry had no wife or children, but lived alone and liked it, signing his email Harry the Hermit. He had his ham-radio license and kept in touch with friends all over the world. Francesca wrote a column about him a few years ago, and the three of us celebrated Thanksgiving together, for as long as I can remember. She called him her honorary grandfather, which he loved, his thin skin flushing with pride.

Harry was a delight to have at a holiday dinner, a former engineer whose conversation was peppered with references to politics, nature, and an ancient tabby cat he adored, named Spunky. Francesca and I used to worry about how Harry would survive when Spunky died, but it turns out he didn't have to, and that's bitter and sweet, too.

Francesca cried when I told her the news, over the phone, and we both talked about how we can't imagine being at the table, without him. We remembered the Thanksgiving we tried to fix him up with Mother Mary, and how my mother broke the conversational ice:

"So, Harry, how many times do you go to the bathroom at night?"

Harry answered, "Mary, more times than I can count."

He never missed a beat, either.

We'll miss him for that, and for so many more reasons, and we're both feeling sad, and happy, and, well, bittersweet.

But we'll give special thanks for having known Harry, and for having him as long as we did.

Life is all the more precious because it doesn't last forever. We learn that over time, and not just in an academic way, but at soul level.

We live that lesson.

At the same time we're with each other, we're losing each other. Time isn't a piece of string with a beginning and an end, not when it's a lifetime. Then, it's an overlay on the present, so that the past is with us always, as is the future.

We're always taking the good with the bad.

We live the pain of the loss at the pleasure of the meeting.

The day I lost Harry, I remembered the day I first saw him, walking on the road. He took me up to his house and showed me the wiring he'd rigged through the trees for his ham radio and the pulley system he invented to feed his fish in a little pond. All of it, his own design.

He didn't want a funeral, and I think I know why.

He designed his life, and his death, too.

He was loved by many, including Francesca and me.

And for him, we are thankful.

For each other, we are thankful.

Happy Thanksgiving.

You will taste the bitter, but may you savor the sweet.

Plan C

• • • • • • • • • • • • • • •

By Lisa

Our Thanksgiving was like no other, complete with a surprise ending.

To give you some background, Francesca and I had been on book tour, going to local stores to sign our previous book, *Best Friends, Occasional Enemies*. I think all of our books make a great gift for the holidays because they're funny.

After all, who doesn't need a laugh, especially around the holidays?

Me, especially.

Here's why.

We recently lost our friend Harry, and we knew our holiday would be a little downcast without him. We were doing okay until Mother Mary called. Of course, we exchanged our Happy-Thanksgiving wishes, then she asked:

"How's Harry?"

Uh-oh.

I hadn't told Mother Mary about Harry yet. Okay, to be honest, I'm not sure I was rushing to give her the news. I knew it would break her heart, and I was waiting for the right moment.

By the way, when is the right moment to break your mother's heart?

On the plus side, I know she'd never find out because she doesn't read the column. There are reruns of *Everybody Loves Raymond* to watch.

And in her defense, and mine, she doesn't read much of anything anymore, so she would have no way of knowing about Harry. But I had to answer her question, and I didn't lie:

"He's not here," I told her.

And none of you are allowed to tell her, either.

Deal?

And in other unfinished business, many of you have written to Francesca and me asking what happened to Harry's beloved cat, Spunky.

Well, we all got the answer to that on Thanksgiving, too.

Harry had arranged for Spunky to be adopted, but my neighbor called me on Thanksgiving to say that the plans had fallen through and that Spunky needed a new home. Apparently, the plan was that the vet would find Spunky a new home, but as it was turning out, there weren't many takers. Spunky is fourteen or so and has a few health problems and you get the idea.

Spunky isn't so spunky anymore.

He's a vet bill on four legs.

So you know where this is going.

The neighbor wanted me to take Spunky.

And so did Francesca.

We discussed it over the holiday meal of buttery brussels sprouts, candied yams, and other saturated fats. I said, "I feel bad for Spunky, but we already have two cats, remember? Mimi and Vivi?"

"But we have room for another," Francesca answered, though she wisely didn't mention that at that very moment, Mimi was jumping up on the chair and making a swipe for a turkey leg.

You haven't lived until you've fought your own cat for a

meal. I cannot have a bowl of cereal without a cat staring me in the face. Same with cheddar cheese, vanilla ice cream, or anything else I'm not supposed to eat.

Cats are portion control with fur.

But to stick with the story, I lifted Mimi off the table. "Plus, what if Spunky didn't get along with Mimi and Vivi? They already hate each other."

Francesca had to admit that much was true. Mimi and Vivi are more than occasional enemies. They've raised cat fighting to an art form. Right now they've achieved a peace as stable as the Greek economy.

Francesca said, "They'll get used to each other."

I considered it. "But what about the dogs? Spunky never lived with a dog."

Welcome, Spunky!

"He can stay upstairs, like the cats do."

Which was also true. The cats stay on the second floor during the daytime, set off by a gate. At night, when the dogs and I go upstairs, the cats go downstairs. Actually now that I tell it, it's a living arrangement that makes a lot of sense. If I'd had done that during my marriage, I wouldn't be divorced.

I still wasn't sure. "But do you really think we're the best home for him?"

Mimi jumped up on the table again, but stayed at the other end, crouching, keeping her own counsel. I couldn't tell if she was listening, and I didn't ask. I tore off a piece of turkey and gave it to her.

Francesca grinned. "I take it that's a yes."

And of course, she was right. We can take care of Spunky.

Got you covered, Harry.

Snow Job

....

By Lisa

Today, we discuss regret. Which I have, in spades, of late.

I don't regret something I bought, which is called buyer's remorse. I regret something I didn't buy, and I don't know what that's called.

Cheapskate's remorse?

Or just plain dumb?

I didn't buy the thing in question because it was expensive and I thought I could do without it, but after doing without it for ten years, I find myself full of regret. I made a mistake. I wish I'd bought one. I yearn for one. I even fantasize about one.

Odd.

I used to lust after men, or jewelry. Thoughts of either could keep me up all night. Men bearing jewelry would be ideal. Men wearing jewelry would not.

But neither of those things is the object of my fantasy, anymore. There's only one thing I don't have that would really turn me on.

Nowadays, my idea of a sex toy is a snowblower.

Oh baby.

I want it so bad, it's good.

But at this point, I'm not sure I can bring myself to buy one. Why?

Regret.

It all started when I was watching the TV news, during the last storm. I love snow coverage, and as soon as there are flurries in the forecast, I switch on the TV. I wait for the anchorman to stand in the middle of the flakes, like a doll in a snowglobe. Or for him to plunge a yardstick into the drift, like a doctor with a thermometer. Or for the Doppler to creep across the map, inching ominously toward us.

Doppler doesn't mess around.

It's *radar.*

But then the storm comes and goes, and the next day on TV, everybody groans and whines as they shovel out their sidewalks, cars, and driveways. There's only one happy person.

The guy with the snowblower.

He's not bent over at all. His hands aren't cramped, and his nose doesn't leak. All he has to do is walk around, with his snowblower doing all the work, parting the drifts like a motorboat in Margate Bay, making a frothy wake.

Oh, yes.

I want one bad.

And I regret that I don't have one, at the same time that I'm not sure whether I should buy one.

I've done without a snowblower for a decade, and I worry that, if I get one now, I'll get the worst of both worlds. If I'd bought it a long time ago, I could've been blowing snow all this time, and gotten one cheaper. Because I didn't, I'll have done without for a decade, and I'll be buying one when it costs more.

It's two for one, mistake-wise.

Regret, regret, regret.

But I kept thinking about getting one, so I went online and studied the websites to make a decision, which is easier said than done. First problem, there are two types of machines, one called a snowblower and one called a snowthrower.

Who knew?

I read the websites, but I couldn't figure out the difference between a snowblower and a snowthrower. I have never blown or thrown snow. I have only shoveled it, scraped it, swept it, and cursed it. I've gotten excellent at cursing it, and done correctly, it won't sprain your back.

Only your middle finger.

I bet you curse snow, too. It rarely responds. I suspect its feelings are hurt. It's used to being wished for, around Christmastime, then oohed and aahed at, even photographed. It remembers when we loved it and called it our winter wonderland.

Then regret sets in, and we regret even the snow.

What happened to those beautiful snowflakes, each one unique?

Who cares?

Die, die, die. Get blown and thrown.

Go away.

The weatherman came on the TV and said there was another storm coming, so I chose the snowblower page and found a grid that let me Shop by Brand, Shop by Type, and Shop by Engine. Then I spotted a category that made it easy:

Shop by In Stock.

Ideal for girls like me.

Who put off buying a snowblower for ten years, and then couldn't take it anymore and drove to the store, saying:

Gimme what you got.

Sell it to me and stick it in my car.

I don't care if it blows, throws, or packs the snow into a cone and squirts it with cherry juice.

I want it gone.

And finally, no regrets.

Lisa Hits the Eggnog

•••••••••••••••••

By Lisa

I love the holidays, because it's the time of the year when we all think about others.

We have no choice.

Even the crabbiest among us has to stop and think about somebody else, because with every gift, we have to ponder what that person really needs, wants, or loves.

It's automatic unselfishness.

That's why I never view gift-giving as commercial. Every harried shopper at the mall just wants to make somebody else happy.

And in so doing, they make themselves happy.

How great is that?

Giving really is getting, and if you want to prove it, watch somebody you love open a gift.

Avoid giving fruitcake.

Or if money is short, give your time. Do somebody a favor. Carry in the groceries. Take out the trash.

Love recycles.

I think that real, profound happiness comes only when you stop thinking about yourself. When you raise your sights, and let your thoughts drift skyward. When you stop focusing on mundane things like how you'll get the cranberry sauce on time or whether you have enough gift cards. When you finally let yourself experience the gratitude, happiness, and peace that wreathe the very air.

This can be an opportunity for reflection, with the old year ending and a new one beginning, the past becoming the future before our very eyes, seamlessly, smooth as a sip of eggnog.

I can never have just one, can you?

Even in troubling times, we can take a few moments to peel back the layers of the everyday and come to understand and appreciate what really matters in life—family and friends.

Like you.

I'm so grateful for all of you, and Daughter Francesca feels the same way.

We've been so thrilled to meet many of you on tour for our new book, and to hear from even more of you via email. As you may know, the book is about the mother-daughter relationship, and many of you have been so open in sharing the joys and bumps of your own mother-daughter relationships, and mother-son relationships, too. Fathers have written to us about their daughters, and vice versa, because love covers all the possible permutations, and is all the same, anyway.

We're all best friends and occasional enemies, aren't we?

Just as love transcends blood ties, it pays no heed to time or space, much less mere geography. So many people can't be with those they love during the holidays because they're overseas at war, serving all of us, and to them, we are most grateful.

They, and their families, are the most unselfish of all.

Others are merely too far away to visit, like Mother Mary and Brother Frank. They won't leave South Beach in December, and who can blame them? She hates the snow, and he hates anyplace you can't wear a muscle shirt.

Many of you have lost those you love, and feel it more acutely at this time of year. My heart goes out to every one of you, and Francesca and I aren't immune to that pain, either. But we take comfort in knowing that our love for those missing from our holiday tables never ends.

It abides, warmly and palpably.

It can make us smile, even now.

Human beings have hearts for such a reason. You may forget your car keys, but you will never forget your mother's smile.

Memories like those are stored in the soul.

And so Francesca and I can recall, at any given moment, what my late father Frank would say about something, or even the silly faces he would make at dinner. For example, when he wanted a second helping, he simply lifted his plate, pointed at the serving dish, and grunted.

It was cuter than it sounds.

But it was really cute.

We used to tease him about it, and he'd laugh, because he was the world's most easygoing person. Nothing really got to him, and I rarely saw him angry. He was a placid, contented man, in a mellow holiday spirit all year round.

Perhaps there's a lesson in that, for his daughter, eh?

I'm Type A, and my father was Type B.

Come to think of it, he was even calmer, like Type C.

Maybe that's Type C, for Christmas?

Maybe.

Lesson learned, Dad.

Happy Holidays, and love, to all.

You Can Never Buy a Gift for a Mother

....

By Lisa

I cheaped out on Mother Mary for Christmas.

I didn't mean to, actually. What really happened was that I gave up. I surrendered. You can't buy a present for Mother Mary without a fistfight.

Here's what happened.

A month before Christmas, I started asking her what she wanted, but I should have known better. Joking aside, she's the best and most unselfish mother on the planet. So I know that she doesn't want me to spend money on her. That she would rather I didn't worry about her. That she would prefer it if I got gifts for Francesca instead. But when I ask her what she wants for Christmas, she keeps those warm and fuzzy sentiments to herself.

What she says to me is, "I don't need anything, I'm half-dead."

I cringe. "Ma, I want to get you a gift. I'm going to get you a gift. So it would help me if you told me something you need."

"I don't need anything."

"Okay, you don't have to need it, you could just want it."

"I don't want anything."

"Come on, Ma. You must want something."

"I want you to not bother getting me a gift!" she says, raising her voice.

"But I *want* to bother," I say, matching her decibel for decibel.

(Actually, the bother is fighting about buying a gift. Fighting about buying a gift takes more time and trouble than buying a gift. In fact, if I had back all the hours I'd spent fighting with my mother about buying her a gift, I would live 189 years.)

"I DON'T WANT A GIFT!" she shouts, angry.

And now I'm angry. "MA, I HAVE TO GET YOU A GIFT! I'LL FEEL GUILTY IF I DON'T GET YOU A GIFT!"

"THAT'S YOUR PROBLEM, COOKIE. NOT MINE."

So you see how it goes. You could say that I should just go out and buy her something nice, and that's what I do every year. I go to a nice jewelry store and get her a necklace or a bracelet. You have to spend money on your mother or you burn in hell. For the Flying Scottolines, hell, guilt, and shame are all big at Christmas.

I buy her the jewelry and send it down to Miami, and she calls me every Christmas morning, after she opens her gift. And she feels guilty. She says, "Honey, why did you do this? I told you not to do this! It cost too much!"

So I console her. "Ma, it didn't cost that much. It's lovely, isn't it? Do you like it? Will you wear it?"

"I love it, but still, I told you not to," she answers.

I know she won't wear it. She never does. She never uses or wears anything I give her. The necklace will stay in her jewelry box, a guilty reminder of the money her daughter spent on her.

See? Guilt. That's the trick at Christmas. The real Christmas gift I give my mother is guilt.

It's one size fits all.

And the price is right.

But I swear to myself, this Christmas will be different. So

last week, I ask Brother Frank what she needs, and he tells me her hearing aids don't work. I call her instantly. "Ma, you need hearing aids. How about I get you a new pair for Christmas?"

"No. I don't need hearing aids."

"Yes, you do. They're broken."

"They're fine."

"No, they're broken. Frank told me. Don't lie."

(This is another gift I give Mother Mary for Christmas. Verbal abuse. Don't try this at home.)

"I didn't lie! Only one is broken!"

Aha! "Okay, sorry."

"So I don't need new hearing aids! I only need one hearing aid! It's not a lie!"

"Okay, okay! So I'll buy one hearing aid. Which one is broken, right or left?"

"They won't sell you one hearing aid," she says, raising her voice.

"Yes, they will," I say.

"NO, THEY WONT!"

"YES, THEY WILL!"

"WRONG!"

"MA, IT'S THE WORST ECONOMY EVER. THEY'LL SELL THEIR MOTHER IF THEY COULD!"

(Why this thought pops into my mind is anyone's guess. Feel free to speculate.)

"THEY WON'T SELL JUST ONE!"

"THEN I'LL BUY TWO AND THROW ONE AWAY!"

So you know where this is going. I bought her one hearing aid for Christmas, which left us both feeling guilty.

Perfect!

You can never buy a gift for your mother.

And oddly, that's as it should be.

All best to you and yours, this holiday.

And Many Happy Returns

· · · · · · · · · · · · · · · ·

By Francesca

Whoever coined the phrase, "and many happy returns," never tried online shopping.

Is there such a thing as a happy return? If I were happy with the item, I'd keep it.

Nobody has intimacy issues with a great gift.

But this is a story about giving gifts, not giving them back.

I love choosing gifts for people, but this year I was under deadline and on a budget, so online shopping seemed like the way to go.

My mom asked for dog sweaters.

You could've guessed that, right?

So I fell into the Internet wormhole of online pet boutiques that sell things like a four-poster cat bed and pearls for dogs. Things only a crazy person would buy.

I wanted all of it.

But I restrained myself. I had a specific objective: three matching dog sweaters in a natural fiber.

Not crazy at all.

I selected my mom's gift in about a half hour. I obsessed over the dogs' gifts for days.

Finally I found a red sweater with a reindeer face on the back. It was adorable, alpaca wool, and had all three sizes in stock. I chose two new harnesses for the big dogs and catnip toys for the cats, including Spunky.

Click click click. Done!

Then, undone.

A week later, I got a call from the company saying the sweaters I ordered were no longer available. Apparently I had chosen the "it" item in canine couture, and it was out of stock.

This bodes well for the economy.

But ill for my Christmas plans.

I'd have to find replacements elsewhere, but my concern was that the rest of the order would go through as scheduled. The customer-service woman assured me nothing had been delayed, and I'd get it all by Christmas.

So I waited.

And worried.

By December 20, only one catnip toy had arrived. That was it. One out of eight items.

Rudolph had better odds.

I called customer service again and got voicemail. I left a message. I called every day from December 21 through 23 and never got a person to pick up. Finally on Friday night, I got a chirpy email from the company saying they were closed for the holiday.

This sparked an artillery of holiday stress. I was incensed. *Oh, just so you're enjoying YOUR holiday while your customers have NOTHING!*

I was going to leave the mother of all voicemails. I'd explain how their website misrepresented their stock, their delivery dates, their quality, and STOLE CHRISTMAS.

I'd have to wait for an opportunity to slip away from my family to unleash on these scam artists.

But then my mom and I went to a packed showing of *The Descendants.*

George Clooney brings people together.

Later that night, I went to a lovely dinner with my dad's family. We had the best time.

I was brushing my teeth when it hit me—I forgot to leave my voicemail bomb.

I told myself it was all right, there was still time for hate. I'd write an email—forceful, articulate, sure to win a compensatory discount. I lay awake in bed drafting it in my head.

Not quite visions of sugarplums.

But then it was Christmas morning. And after the presents were opened, my mom and I got down to the merry business of cooking together. And soon her best friend Franca arrived, and we all ate dinner with the dogs at our feet.

By the twenty-sixth my wrath had cooled. Christmas was over. Some of the missing gifts I'd replaced in time, some I hadn't.

I was too busy enjoying my family, my friends, and my holiday to be disgruntled.

A week later, I still haven't received anything else from the company, but my lesson for the New Year is this:

Anger, even the righteous kind, isn't worth missing out on joy. Make time for the things that give and need love, and let the rest slide.

But when these purchases arrive, I intend to send them right back.

Now that's a happy return.

Happy New Year!

Controlled Freaks

• • • • • • • • • • • • • • • • •

By Lisa

My golden retriever and I are eating food that looks exactly alike. And for almost the same reason.

This can't be good.

But it's delicious.

You may remember that last summer, I tried to lower my cholesterol the natural way, without drugs. That meant I had to lose weight, which was when I discovered that my problem is portion control.

In that I have none.

Please tell me I'm not alone. I can't be, because I've noticed that more and more food marketing is targeted at people like me, in that pretzels, cookies, and chips now come in 100-calorie packs.

This shouldn't work, in principle. If you're on a diet, you shouldn't be eating pretzels, cookies, and chips at all, but evidently, human nature is such that if you can cheat a little, you will.

It doesn't work with marriage.

Only with carbohydrates.

The idea is that it doesn't matter what the food is, just that there's 100 calories of it in the bag, and people like me will permit themselves one bag, but stop short of starting another.

Because they know that if they open another, they'll have to eat that one, too.

I admit, I exploit this fact of human nature, for my books. If I can write something at the end of a chapter that will make a reader start the next chapter, I know their natural inclination will be to read another whole chapter. This is a leftover from our Calvinist notion that you finish what you start, which is great as applied to books, but not as applied to pizza.

Case in point, when I was little, Mother Mary never asked me if I was full. She asked: "Did you make it all gone?"

The answer was, of course, and I still do. And now my waist is all gone.

So in a quest to have my portions controlled for me, I found a product called Morningstar Farms sausage patties. The good news is that they come two to a package, have only 150 calories, and no cholesterol. The bad news is they look like hockey pucks.

They're not real sausages, and that's fine with me. Most pigs are smarter than I am, so I don't mind not eating one. And the patties taste great, though I don't know what's in them and don't really care.

Anyway, every morning for three months, I ate two fake sausages with two egg whites. And at night I ate Bocaburgers, black bean burgers, or veggie burgers, which also look like hockey pucks.

I lost weight, though I didn't lower my cholesterol.

And I felt sure I could ice skate.

Now switch gears to Penny the golden retriever, who's getting older and fatter, and the vet said she needed to lose weight. I went to the pet store and told them my problem.

I mean, Penny's problem. I said to the salesman, "I have an old dog who needs to be on a diet, but she has no portion control."

He handed me a red bag. "Then feed her this. It's beef patties, but raw."

So I bought the dog food, brought it home, and took two patties out of the bag. They're round, flat, and brown, and they look like hockey pucks. If you put them on a plate next to my fake-sausage patties, you could easily mistake the dog food for the people food.

Or think you had invited the Flyers to dinner.

And like the fake-sausage patties, I have no idea what's in the beef patties. It says they're raw, freeze-dried beef, but I don't understand why they don't leave grease or blood all over on my hands. I only know that every day, twice a day, I cut up hockey pucks for Penny, then I cut up hockey pucks for me, and we both enjoy our portion-controlled, vaguely food-like meals.

Who said you can teach an old dog new tricks?

Dating at the Speed Limit,
or the Bad News

· · · · · · · · · · · · · · · · ·

By Lisa

I have good news and bad news about my dating life. First, the bad news. Dating at fifty is exactly the same as dating at fifteen.

Except for the braces.

Yes, I had braces at fifteen, and I'm dating again. I don't know which is worse.

I mean, better.

My friends tell me to have a positive attitude. Take my characteristic upbeat approach. Flip it. In other words, if I hate dating, I have to start liking it.

Presto-chango.

But dating might be the only case where flipping it doesn't work, especially if you're middle-aged. For example, if you touch knees under the table, they're replacement knees.

If you feel titanium pressing against you, it really is titanium.

And when a man tells you to sit on his good side, he means the side on which he hears better, not the side on which he looks better.

And hearing's not the only thing going south. I had a first

date with a man who told me that he'd need an hour's notice if he was going to be "staying over."

You can guess why.

I told him he wasn't staying over.

(And switch to Cialis.)

I don't go out that much, and every time I do go out, it reminds me of why I don't. Dating hasn't changed at all, but I have.

After two divorces, I've lost the completely starry-eyed hope that love conquers all. I know that love isn't enough.

Love is just a good start.

And of course, I believe in love and all that blah blah, but the truth is, it's different now. I hope it can be better, but I have yet to fall in love again.

Stay tuned.

But don't hold your breath.

Because I am.

Here's what I mean. Now, if I'm on a dinner date, I listen for the red flags. I missed so many before, I'm determined not to do that again, so on the date, I'm waiting for the guy to eliminate himself, like waiting for the love shoe to drop.

I'm not having a conversation, I'm evaluating one. My date thinks we're talking, but I'm watching him skip through a minefield, set to explode as soon as he steps a foot wrong. For example, I was recently on a first date with a perfectly nice guy, until he referred to his ex-wife as a bitch.

Ka-boom!

All I heard was an explosion.

If he still hates his ex, he's out. I know this sounds hypocritical, because I'm not a huge fan of my own exes. But I call them Thing One and Thing Two, not worse. I'm out of love with them, and equally importantly, I'm out of hate.

By the way, if he still loves his ex-wife, he's out, too. This came up on another first date, when the guy kept referring to his "wife and kids."

Finally, I asked, "You're divorced, right?"

"Yes, sure," he answered. And he had been for five years.

Ka-boom!

Generally I'm at the point where I know that talking about the past is no-win, because I have a lot of past, and so does anyone my age. If we start talking about it, we'll never get to the present by dessert. After all, there's only so much time at dinner, and I can break it down for you:

The first ten minutes of any date are spent going for our respective reading glasses, and we whip them out like a showdown for the superannuated.

The man is usually the quicker draw, because he isn't worried about what he looks like in reading glasses. I fumble for mine, act casual as I put them on, and suppress the inner voice that says, Men Don't Make Passes at Girls Who Wear Reading Glasses.

So far, so good.

Then we have to get the waitress's attention, to order, which presents another test my hapless date doesn't know he's taking. Because I'm used to getting the waitress myself, since that's what single women learn to do.

Or they starve.

It's not hard to get a waitress's attention. Make eye contact, dude. Waitresses don't like to be waved at, and I know.

I was one.

Yet I restrain myself and don't call the waitress myself. If my date cannot succeed in doing so for fifteen minutes, he's out.

Ka-boom!

Because I'm hungry, and I can't take it.

To be fair, I set up the mine only because you're damned if you do, and damned if you don't. I was on a date once where the guy couldn't get the waitress's attention, so I did, and his face fell. Later, when we walked to our respective cars, he remarked that my car was nicer than his. And I knew I was getting the kiss of death, instead of a kiss goodnight.

What's a girl to do?

Keep the car, and get a higher-octane guy.

Skype Appeal

· · · · · · · · · · · · · · · · ·

By Francesca

Dating a person with an accent is the best thing ever. There's only one drawback.

They're not from here.

My British boyfriend and I had spent five blissful months together in New York City. The foreign aspect of him manifested in only the most charming details, like drinking tea instead of coffee, taking toast with Marmite, and complimenting my "bum."

But then he told me he'd have to spend some time back home for work, and his connection to a place thousands of miles away became a stark reality.

And so I was introduced to the savior and scourge of every long-distance relationship: Skype.

Skype is a free, Internet-based program that lets you "call" and video-chat with anyone anywhere in the world. It sounds awesome. In many ways it is. But in others, it's a Trojan horse of romantic woes.

We planned Skype dates, although I use the word "plan" lightly. With a time difference and completely different schedules, we took whatever time together we could get. Normally, the program displays which of your friends are available to call, but my boyfriend kept his status "invisible" so his hundred other Skype contacts wouldn't bother him when we were talking.

He was my only Skype contact.

So he initiated all of our calls. That meant I had to be camera-ready at any moment. This was not going to be easy.

Not that I could tell him that.

I work at home, so I rarely look appropriate for public consumption, much less boyfriend consumption. My daily uniform is some variation of workout clothes, regardless of whether or not I make it to the gym. If I think I'll have to go out, I might wear old jeans, but that's as good as it gets on a weekday.

Imagine a twenty-five-year-old woman styled by Kevin James.

I don't bother with makeup at home, and I conserve my One-A-Day contact lenses like the gold that they are. Unless I'm going on a date, I'm wearing my glasses.

Looking casually beautiful twenty-four/seven was going to be a full-time job.

I asked my friend, who has also had a long-distance boyfriend in another time zone, for styling advice. "Go full-on painted whore," she said. "There's no such thing as too much eye makeup on Skype."

I tried it, going for a Kim Kardashian level of artificial perfection. In the mirror, I looked like a rejected cast member of *Jersey Shore,* fired on account of paleness. But on my computer's built-in camera, the makeup looked all right, in a Fem-bot sort of way.

Still, I didn't feel like myself. So I washed it off and settled for nighttime eyeliner.

Then I scouted my entire apartment for which spots had the best light at each time of day.

Morning: at my table, facing the kitchen window.

Afternoon: in my bedroom, facing the setting sun.

Evening: on the couch, facing the better lamp, with the laptop on a pillow.

This way, whenever he called, I could stop, drop, and roll into optimal position before activating the camera function.

Meanwhile, my boyfriend would call me while lying on his sofa with the laptop on his belly and the camera aiming up his nose. He was completely unself-conscious.

It was one of the things I found most adorable about him.

And yes, I recognize the irony.

Using the thing has its own pitfalls. The camera eye is at the tippy-top of your computer screen, but the image of your friend appears on the screen below, which means you can't look at the lens and your friend at the same time. In other words, you're watching each other watch each other.

It's all very meta.

And painfully self-conscious; it's like being thirteen all over again.

I'm not this girl. Well, I was this girl, but I grew out of her.

Should your vanity get the best of you, Skype provides you with a rearview mirror of sorts, an auxiliary window that shows you the image of yourself, as seen by your partner. This smaller window appears beside the main one, serving as constant temptation to check yourself out.

The trouble is, if you're sneaking peeks all the time, your partner will see your shifty eyes.

Rapid eye movement is not sexy.

Talking on Skype, I felt sapped of my powers, my mojo, my wiles. My go-to style of flirting is to make jokes. But Skype can be glitchy, and there's often a delay on the video feed, so our usual banter was reduced to talking over each other with a sprinkling of awkward pauses.

And God forbid I try and be funny. Thanks to the delay, my jokes would be followed by a moment of absolutely no reaction.

In reality, it was probably a two-second break, but in my mind, that was plenty of time to panic:

Omigod, Francesca, you are such an idiot. Why did you say that?

Maybe he didn't hear it, should I say it again?

Or no, just pretend it didn't happen.

Okay, it didn't happen.

Only then he would laugh.

But still, I missed my boyfriend more than I disliked myself on camera, so I always looked forward to our calls. Little by little, I followed his lead and relaxed. My favorite was when he would play guitar for me over Skype, because that felt less like watching a video and more like being together.

We settled into a nightly routine of Skyping each other.

Sometimes I even wore my glasses.

I was getting the hang of it when disaster struck in the form of good news. He'd been offered a terrific full-time job . . . over there. So he wouldn't be coming back to "the States" after all.

If I thought I looked less than perfect on Skype before, watching myself cry on camera cured me of that notion. I felt crummy enough, I really didn't need to see my snot bubbles on screen.

There's a *Sex and the City* episode about Carrie getting dumped via Post-It, but that's nothing compared to breaking up over Skype. It has all the embarrassment of a face-to-face breakup with none of the physical comfort. You're robbed of the bittersweet breakup hug. And if you're splitting on less-than-amicable terms, you definitely shouldn't throw a drink in his face.

But our breakup was amicable, just three thousand miles apart.

I suppose having your ex across an ocean does offer certain assurances, like we'll never bump into each other when I least expect it.

No matter how much I'd like to.

Dating at the Speed Limit,
or the Good News

• • • • • • • • • • • • • • • • •

By Lisa

The good is that dating at my age can be as fun as dating when I was sixteen years old. It's still thrilling to kiss someone new, though it's equally surprising to find myself, even at my age, worrying about it all through dinner.

Part of the problem is logistics. Most of my dates involve meeting someone at a restaurant, so that means there'll be a goodnight kiss in some guaranteed-awkward location. Namely, a suburban parking lot.

Good night, Irene.

I freeze up. I don't like it. Families are walking by, and nobody feels sexy around minivans.

Worse, some of the restaurants have valets, usually a bright-eyed young man who has nowhere to go after he opens the car door for you. The last time this happened on a date, I gave my date a peck and almost gave one to the valet, standing next to him like an earnest son.

And there was another time when my date walked me to my car, which was parked around the back of the restaurant. As we approached my car, I saw a group of busboys taking their cigarette breaks in front of my grille. Again, I stiffened, but my date was fine with it, like a host in front of a studio audience. He went to kiss me, and I recoiled.

"Really?" I asked.

Which is not the kind of thing that most men like to hear when they're zooming in for the smooch. But this guy took it in stride.

"Just ignore them," he said, but I couldn't, then oddly, as if on cue, the busboys put out their cigarettes and shuffled inside the kitchen, evidently following the secret rules of some Guy Code. But by then, the air was filled with carcinogens, and the moment had gone up in a puff of smoke.

The truth is, that all of this is an excuse. Because I'm worrying that I forget how to kiss.

I know, it's embarrassing to admit this in print, but we know I tell the truth in these essays, and why stop now.

I can't be the only one who forgets how to kiss.

A guy I mean.

I can kiss a dog, no problem. I kiss their lips, heads, ears, and paws. Easy as pie. Piece a cake.

Also cats. I'm a great cat kisser. They keep coming back for more.

As long as I hold them down.

I kiss horses, too, and their noses are all big and velvety.

So you would think I can kiss a guy, because they're not as big as a horse, as feisty as a cat, or as sloppy as a dog.

But no.

I forget.

It's not like riding a bike; it's like learning a language. If you don't use it, you lose it. In other words, if you don't practice your French, you forget how to French.

Which brings me to the subject of tongues.

Just when I thought I was getting the hang of the goodnight kiss, someone tried to slip me the tongue. On our first kiss ever. In his car.

I jumped back so far it almost qualified as a secondary collision.

Dude, only my dogs get tongue.

Which brings me to an even more personal subject.

Sex.

You've heard the folklore that it's okay to sleep with someone after three dates, but I think that's crazy.

Unless he's George Clooney.

For a normal guy, three dates is too soon. I don't sleep with someone until I'm in love, and I haven't been in love for a long time, if you follow. The odd thing is, to be completely honest, I've gotten some pushback on the issue.

As in whining.

By which I mean, I recall one date where the guy was miffed that I wouldn't sleep with him, saying, "Come on, it's not like we're kids anymore."

Really?

I'm not sure I follow. I may be in my fifties, but I still have feelings. And there has to be a better line than telling a woman she should sleep with you because she's too old to matter.

I still link sex with love, maybe even more than when I was younger. I value everything more these days, and yes, I value myself more.

Funny, in a way, that guy was right.

I'm not a kid anymore, dude.

And that's why I'm not sleeping with *you*.

Girl with a Pearl Earring

• • • • • • • • • • • • • • • •

By Lisa

It all started when I went into my jewelry box for a pair of earrings and found four teeth.

Let me explain.

My jewelry box is a mess. None of the earrings is with its mate, which is the story of my life. Even my earrings are single.

My hoops are hopeless.

I was trying to find a pearl earring, which was lost amid a tangle of gold chains, bound tight as a rubber-band ball, and a slew of earring backs, strewn around like so many tiny Mickey Mouse ears.

It's as if I don't value my valuables.

Please tell me I'm not alone in this.

The problem is that my jewelry box contains every piece of jewelry I've ever owned, even a happy-face ring that Mother Mary gave me when I was ten years old.

Do you know anybody *less* likely to give a happy-face ring than Mother Mary? I showed it to her once, and she denied having bought it.

I think she was trying to save happy face.

I kept my first pair of gold posts, still scabby, from sixth grade, when I used to drown my newly pierced ears in alcohol, so I smelled vaguely like a pathology lab. I spent most of the school day turning my posts, panicked that the holes would close up.

This was in the old days, when the only thing people pierced was their earlobes. I wonder if people with pierced nipples have to turn them.

Their earrings, not their nipples.

Either way, serves them right.

I also have spoon-handle earrings from my hippie days in high school, which continue, in that I'm still hippy.

I have silver bangles from the years I loved silver, and gold bangles from when I got my first credit card. These things are not unrelated.

I have a high school ring, a college ring, and two wedding rings.

Two of these things make me smile.

And the other two make me laugh.

Most of my jewelry box isn't jewelry, but random stuff. It's as if my jewelry box had an affair with my junk drawer and gave birth to an array of foreign money, Mass cards, and old laminated driver's licenses.

This would be the trifecta of things no woman can throw away.

I can't throw away foreign money, because after all, it's still money.

Except for the euros. I hear that's not money anymore.

I have coins from Australia because I never know when I'll be in Australia again.

And when that day comes, I'll bring my thirty-seven Australian cents.

Then there are Mass cards. Sadly, I have more Mass cards than times I've been to Mass.

For those of you who aren't Catholic, a Mass card is sent to notify you that prayers are being said for someone who has passed. I can't throw one away, though I have Mass cards for people I don't remember and never even knew. I even have Mass cards that were sent to me by mistake.

Still, I'm not throwing away a Mass card. That would be like throwing people away. And I can't throw away an old driver's license, because that would be like throwing *me* away.

In the bottom of the jewelry box were four baby teeth from Francesca, three wrapped in old toilet paper, but one loose, a cute nugget of little-girl ivory. I remembered the day she lost the tooth, after dinner, in an orange. The Tooth Fairy left her twenty dollars because it was all she had in her wallet and the bank was closed.

The teeth were with Francesca's baby bracelet from the hospital, a plastic ring not wide enough for two fingers, which read Baby Girl Scottoline.

She still is that, to me.

And there was a lock of her baby hair, thin and gold, with a single curl like an oversized comma.

I held the teeth, bracelet, and hair in my hand, trying to decide whether to clean up the jewelry box.

It was my life, after all, with the valuable, invaluable, and just plain absurd mixed up together.

So I closed the lid, and let it be.

Magic Mushrooms

. . . .

By Francesca

My mom got me dirt for Christmas.

At least that's what it looked like at first. Then she explained that it was an at-home mushroom-growing kit.

"FUN FOR KIDS!" it said across the box.

Or for your twenty-five-year-old daughter!

But who am I kidding? I was super excited to play with the kit.

The kit is an upright rectangular box with a little trapdoor that reveals a plastic bag inside. The plastic bag looks like it contains rotting compost, but it's actually recycled coffee grounds and mushroom seeds. The directions said all you have to do is cut a slit in the bag, soak it overnight, and mist it with water twice a day, and—voila!—you're a gourmet-mushroom farmer.

I like some plant matter in my apartment. I grow fresh sage, rosemary, basil, and thyme in a pot on my windowsill. But since I cut most meat from my diet, I hardly use the herbs, so at this point, the plant is taking over my windowsill.

Whatever, it looks pretty.

And I support the green movement. Apparently mushrooms are normally grown on wood chips, so this kit saves trees and recycles old coffee waste. The company website says they're on track to redirect 1 million pounds of used coffee grounds.

I get saving trees, but I had no idea coffee waste was such a threat. Are we in danger of caffeine rain?

So I set up shop. If it was meant for kids, how hard could it be? For the first week, absolutely nothing happened. If you want to test your patience, wait for a plant to grow. I felt like an idiot, dutifully misting the outside of a plastic bag, but I had faith.

On the fifth day, my patience was rewarded. The following is a daily log of my mushrooms' growth.

Day 5: What I found in my kitchen looked like something you'd find on a foot. I thought it was going to look like a munchkin colony of perfectly formed baby mushrooms, like the way a baby snail is a perfect miniature of its mother.

But what I saw today was the Rosemary's Baby of mushroom plants. It didn't even look like a plant, just a bumpy protrusion, or the type of wart you definitely need to get looked at.

It was unappetizing, to say the least.

I frowned and misted twice.

Day 6: Holy! These babies are twice as big as they were yesterday and, more frightening, they've multiplied. I've got what looks like a million of them. It's a mushroom metropolis. Their roots are forming a subway system.

And did you know the mushroom seeds aren't called seeds, but "spawn"? That's kind of concerning, right? I needed this information six days ago.

Nervous, I checked the website, where the end-result photos show a much more reasonable number of caps, ten to fifteen, so I can only assume these wicked mushrooms eat their young. That, or it's a *Lord of the Flies* scenario where only the strong survive.

Lord of the Fungi.

Or maybe I just have an overachieving fungus.

I'm almost proud.

Day 6½: I take that back—I'm disturbed. They're bigger

than they were this morning. And by the way, I'm only getting my 4 P.M. coffee.

Day 7: They're taking over! This rapid growth is out of control. I go out to walk my dog and by the time I come back, they're a little bit larger. I find myself creeping over to the mushroom garden several times a day and peering at it with suspicion, inspecting it for signs of movement.

What kind of space plant have I allowed into my home?

Any minute I'm going to hear, "Feed me, Seymour!"

I risked allowing the creature near my face when I put my ear up to it to see if I could hear it crackling, popping, grumbling with growth. But I heard nothing.

It's not so foolish as that.

I imagined the mushroom tentacles advancing when my back is turned, but just when I look at it, they freeze again.

Heedless of my better judgment, I continue to water it. I feel like Dr. Frankenstein.

Day 8: I learned something today: A fungus is not a plant. I should say relearned, because I'm sure my high school biology teacher taught this, but all I remember of him is that he was very young, very nervous, and completely abused by us. He was only at our school for one year, after which I'm afraid we drove him to some terrible fate.

Like law school.

Somehow, nine years and a Harvard degree later, my command of science remains at, "Is it a plant, 'er is it a critter?"

With apologies to any botany geeks I've been annoying thus far, I now know that a mushroom is neither plant nor critter, but it is a living organism.

I find this very confusing. I was just getting used to the concept that yogurt has "live active cultures" in it.

Calm down, yogurt, I'm not even that live active most days. But it's true: Fungi lack chlorophyll to feed themselves through photosynthesis, so they're classified in a separate kingdom from green plants. But fungi can't ingest their food like animals either. Instead, they absorb it.

These freaks get their own kingdom!

But now it all makes sense—the "spawn," the sneaky, creeping growth.

Do you think it knows I'm planning to "harvest" it?

Day 9: Either the mushrooms are growing more beautiful, or I'm developing Stockholm Syndrome, but somehow I have

"My pretties."

had a change of heart. Checking on the mushrooms is now my favorite activity of the day.

Now that they're larger, it's easier to see how amazing they are. All the caps have a cute little dimple at the top where they still need to fill out. Their curved necks are bedecked with a fan of pleats, as if each one is wearing an Elizabethan collar. Some still carry the blue cast of their babyhood, while others are maturing to a warm brown.

I'm this close to naming them.

Day 10: My little babies are all grown-up! They grow up so fast. I'm glad I kept this mushroom baby diary for them to read later. I'll edit out the parts where I called them spawn.

Now I adore them. Every morning, I touch their spongy heads, and it feels like a wet doggie nose.

Wait, what?

I have to chop them, cook them, and eat them?

Don't talk like that.

Not in front of the mushrooms.

I would never have cut it in 4-H.

These are beautiful, a miracle of nature on my kitchen counter. Buy these for your kids, or pretend you have kids and buy these for yourself.

Just don't give them names.

Mythical Beastie

· · · · · · · · · · · · · · · ·

By Lisa

I know I've written about my feet before, but changes are afoot.

Sorry.

To begin, my feet barely look human anymore. My soles have thickened to an elephant's hide, and my toenails have turned to horn, curved and yellowing.

I don't have feet, I have hooves.

Bottom line, I'm becoming a centaur. Or maybe a Minotaur. Either way, I'm not getting remarried anytime soon.

Unless Thing Three is the Old Spice guy.

To top it off, my amazing disappearing little toenail is now long gone. I guess it was vestigial. I think it dissolved into my sock when I was fifty-one or so, but I forget.

Turns out that memory is vestigial, too.

I suppose a pedicure would solve these foot problems, but I generally ignore them. I don't want to inflict my feet on a salon, which probably lacks the requisite nuclear weaponry.

But now there's something about my feet that I can't ignore.

First, a warning.

The following may be an overshare, but why stop now? Overshare is my middle name. Besides, how can sharing too much ever be wrong? It's the season of giving, so here goes:

I have a bunion.

You know what that is? The Internet will give you the medical details, but all I know is that a few years ago, that big bone on the side of my foot started growing sideways, completing my transformation into a gargoyle.

Nobody told me that in my middle age, I would turn into something from the Middle Ages.

But as you know, I try to look on the bright side. For example, I'll be more stable on a windy day, now that my foot is sprouting a foot. I'll be harder to knock over now, though I bet nobody will try. They'd be afraid I'd bite them with my pointy teeth or fly at them on leathery wings.

I'm cranky, for a mythical beast. After all, I'm a menopausal mythical beast.

But to stick to the story, I ignored my bunion for as long as I could, which means until all my fancy shoes couldn't fit anymore. I'm lucky enough to have quite a few pairs of nice shoes, which I save for signings and dates.

Okay, mostly for signings.

But a bunion renders all those great shoes unwearable. In other words, a peep toe is sexy. A peep bunion is not.

Plus it's straight-up unfair of your body to be growing something new, at this point in life. Middle age is already undignified enough, with waistlines widening willy-nilly and chins sprouting hair, like bamboo for the face. Now, my bones are stretching my skin.

Which is my fat's job.

Honestly, if I get stretch marks, I want it to be from chocolate cake.

So I went to the doctor's for my annual exam, and he took one look at my right foot, frowning. "You can't keep ignoring this bunion," he said, gently.

"I can't?" I asked, then I corrected myself. "I agree, I can't.

But why?" I didn't explain that I ignore everything bad, in the hope that it will go away.

This works, but only with husbands.

The doctor continued, "If you deal with it now, you can avoid general anesthesia. You can get a local block."

"You mean I need surgery?"

"Yes." The doctor pointed to my second toe. "See how your big toe is shifting over and taking up the room where your second toe should be? If you don't fix this, in time, your second toe will be on top of your big toe. That's called hammertoe."

I tried not to vomit in my mouth.

"This may run in your family," said the doctor.

Then I remembered that all of my aunts wore bedroom slippers everywhere, even to weddings. One aunt even had dress flip-flops, for funerals.

The Flying Scottolines keep it classy.

So by the time you read this, I should have gone under the knife and will have to stay off my feet for seven weeks.

But I'm looking on the bright side. I have a new book to write and I like sitting.

God willing, I'm going to earn some stretch marks.

Blizzard of Oz

· · · · · · · · · · · · · · · · ·

By Lisa

I've been nesting like crazy lately, which is funny considering that I have no eggs left.

I can't explain this, but I'm betting that I'm not the only Mama Bird who looked around her empty nest and realized that it needed curtains.

At first I dismissed the idea. I thought it made no sense, timing-wise. I've had no curtains, on any of the windows, for the past twenty years. Why fix up the house now that it was empty? The horse had not only left the barn, she had moved to New York.

Then I realized that I still lived here, and I still count, even though no one is peeping inside my windows to see me, except a bird or two, and a really desperate squirrel.

But I have bats in the shutters outside my bedroom window, and that's reason enough to get curtains. The bats aren't looking at me, but I'm looking at them, and it's spooky. I see them when they fly, squeaking, at night, like the winged monkeys in the *Wizard of Oz*.

I'm the wicked witch, of course. She used to terrify me when I was little, but now I relate. It's hard to say when in life we stop identifying with Dorothy and start identifying with the witch, but my guess is:

Now.

Sometimes I stand at the window and call to the bats, "Now, fly! Fly!"

Also the witch was a shoe fan, like me. She even says to the monkey, "Take special care of those ruby slippers! I want those most of all!"

The *Wizard of Oz* was a movie about two women fighting over a pair of pumps.

This happens every day at a Nordstrom's shoe sale, but goes unremarked.

You may remember that my curtain renaissance began after the decorating debacle of the family room, where the yellow curtains came dotted with black spots that looked like pre-toxic mold. In the end, the company agreed the fabric was defective, and I learned to love again. In fact, I found a new curtain maker who came over, measured my windows, and is already on the case. But when I imagined the nice, new curtains against the scuffy walls, I realized that the walls needed painting. And then I looked again and realized that nobody could paint anything with the room so messy, so I started cleaning.

This is why you should never actually look around your house.

You see things.

And I realized that if I wanted new curtains, I had to clean my entire house, and I couldn't clean after my bunion surgery, so I got busy.

Also, if I died in surgery, at least my house would be clean. Everybody would say "she kept a nice house," when they came over after the funeral. My tombstone could read, SHE REALLY WASN'T THAT MUCH OF A PIG.

So I started by cleaning my family room, then moved on to my office, my bedroom, and my laundry room. Yes, even the laundry room, where gravity is the hamper.

I picked up all the dirty clothes and even went through all the sheets falling out of the shelves. The sheets don't fit on the shelves because there are way too many, leftover from beds of bygone days, and even past marriages. You know you don't clean enough when you find ex-sheets on the shelves.

I wanted to burn them, but settled for throwing them away.

The laundry-room shelves are a mess because nobody can fold a fitted sheet, not even Tom Cruise. Folding a fitted sheet is Mission Impossible, so I always roll them up into a ball and stuff them onto the shelf. This time I tried to make smaller balls, in case my mourners came upstairs.

Then I cleaned my bedroom closet.

It took me eight hours of sorting through old shirts and sweaters, and even skirts. I can't remember the last time I wore a skirt. Soon, skirts will become extinct, like slips and sanitary belts.

Moment of silence for the sanitary belt.

Even though it wasn't sanitary.

Finally, I sorted the filthy mound of shoes at the bottom of my closet, setting aside muddy clogs and ancient Frye boots until I found a pair of black pumps I'd been looking for for ten years.

Not exactly the ruby slippers, but close enough.

And wearable when I get my new feet.

Fly!

Mother Mary and the MRI

• • • • • • • • • • • • • • • •

By Lisa

Mother Mary tells me on the phone that they're building giant red condominiums across the street from her house.

"Really?" I ask her, confused. Her street is a small, quiet backstreet, the last of its kind in South Beach.

"Yes," she answers. "I can see it outside the window. New red condos. They're ugly."

"But there are houses there. What about the houses? Did they tear them down?"

"I don't see them."

This makes no sense. "And the condos are red?"

"Bright red."

I don't like the sound of this, and suddenly I lose my sense of humor. "Put Frank on the phone, okay?"

So she does, and my brother picks up. "I know, right?" he says, and it's all he has to say, because he sounds worried, too.

"There aren't really condos, are there?" I ask.

"No, and she thinks everything's red."

"You mean she's seeing red? Literally?"

"Yes."

It would be funny, if my sense of humor came back. Mother Mary has been seeing red her whole life.

So we're both worried she had some kind of ministroke,

though I have no idea what kind of stroke causes you to see red condos. If I had a stroke, I'd see Bradley Cooper. And he can be whatever color he likes, because he's the new George Clooney.

So Frank takes Mother Mary to the doctor, who finds nothing wrong but schedules her for an MRI, and we know right away that this is a problem.

Mother Mary hates MRIs.

First, she hates small spaces. Second, she hates hospitals. Third, she hates most things.

She hasn't had an MRI for years, when she was getting radiation for throat cancer. She beat the cancer, though it left her with some throat issues, but she still hated the trips to the hospital, and I don't really blame her, but I get her on the phone.

"Mom, you have to get an MRI. We have to see if something's wrong with you."

"No."

"You have to go. It's doctor's orders." Never mind that it was doctor's orders to use her oxygen, which she also ignored, and I'm wondering if this is why she's seeing red. "Please go, for me."

"No."

"What about for Frank?"

"Maybe," she answers, then laughs.

Long story short, my brother convinces her to get the MRI, and I call to see how it went.

Mother Mary answers, "I don't want to talk about it."

"What do you mean?" I ask, alarmed. "What happened?"

"I *said,* I don't want to talk about it."

I have no idea if this means something is really wrong, because nothing is drama-free with Mother Mary, especially not drama. "Put Frank on, okay?"

So she does, and he tells me that she didn't have the MRI at all, because of what happened.

Drama. To wit:

He accompanies her into the MRI room while they slide her into the MRI machine. She lies down, and they give her a rubber ball to squeeze if she gets panicky. Frank hears her clear her throat a few times, then all of a sudden he sees the rubber ball fly across the room. The MRI technician doesn't see this. Frank starts yelling, and they slide her out of the machine, where she was choking from fluid that blocked her throat.

"What fluid?" I ask him, horrified.

"Since the radiation, when she lies down too long, fluid builds up in her throat."

"What about when she sleeps?"

"She moves around then, I guess."

"Why didn't she squeeze the ball, like they told her?"

"She did, but her grip wasn't strong enough for it to register. That's why she threw it."

I picture the scene, shaken. "So did she really almost choke?"

"Honestly, yes."

I feel awful for her. "She must have been terrified."

"To be real, she was pissed." Frank chuckles. "I think she was trying to throw the ball at the technician."

That sounds like her. "So now what?"

"They said she needs an upright MRI."

"Think she'll go?"

"We'll make her."

"How?"

"We'll do what we always do," Frank answers. "You nag her, and I'll use my feminine wiles."

I smile.

I love my brother, because he never loses his sense of humor, and for many other reasons.

God bless the caregivers, especially Mother Mary's.

Grandmother Whisperer

· · · · · · · · · · · · · · · ·

By Francesca

They call me The Grandmother Whisperer.

Grandmothers are complicated, sensitive creatures. You can't "break" a grandmother's spirit, nor should you try to. That spirit has been around two, three, maybe four times as long as yours has.

And Mother Mary is no exception.

Every whisperer has a stunt to show the true extent of his or her influence. Cesar Milan will bring an unleashed pit bull to calm an aggressive Chihuahua; Buck Brannaman will get a wild mustang to lie down on its side. And I will tell you how I entered the ring, or "kitchen," with my untamed grandmother, and, using the following gentle guidelines, took over the cooking of Eggplant Parmesan.

Mother Mary was recently staying with us while she had work done to her house in Miami, and my mom had been begging her to make us her famous Eggplant Parmesan.

"C'mon Ma, if you're here, we're gonna put you to work!" Mom joked.

My grandmother flung an arm out to swat her.

It's attitudes like this that get people hurt.

Rule Number 1 of grandmother husbandry: Appeal to their innate sense of hierarchy.

"I'd love to learn how to make eggplant parm," I said. "Can you teach me?"

Minutes later, we were heating up oil.

My grandmother explained the first steps, but she's such a pro, her teaching style tends to be doing it all herself with narration. And although my mother was the one who wanted the eggplant parm in the first place, she had a lot of . . . suggestions. Things like:

"Not too much salt!" and "Don't overcook them, Ma, you like them cooked to death."

I could tell the only thing getting overheated was Mother Mary.

Which leads me to Rule Number 2: Be calm-assertive, but let her think she's in charge.

"Here," I said, gently slipping the utensils from my grandmother's hands. "Let me try it myself or I'll never learn. You relax, then judge when I'm finished, okay?"

"Okay, kitten," she said, and shuffled over to preside at the kitchen island.

And so commenced a fairly peaceful cooking session with all three generations in the same kitchen.

I had just lifted the last slice of golden brown breaded eggplant from the fryer, when I asked for Mother Mary's approval. "How do they look?"

But my grandmother didn't look up.

"Ma," my mom said loudly, catching her attention. "Please, put in your hearing aids."

"Why." My grandmother is the only person who can say this word without a question mark.

"Because I want you to hear what we're saying."

"Maybe I don't want to listen."

"I'm serious. I'm tired of yelling."

"You yell anyway!"

Rule Number 3: Do not attempt to outwit the grandmother. This is impossible.

"They make no difference," added Mother Mary.

"They make a difference to us, to your family. Put them in right now, please."

Rule Number 4: Don't bark orders; listen and respond.

"Mom, wait," I said. "What if she means 'they make no difference' as in, they don't work? Maybe there's something wrong with them." I turned to my grandmother, and asked, "Can I try them?"

My grandmother looked surprised.

My mom looked disgusted. "You're going to put them in your ears?" my mom asked. "That's so gross."

This coming from the woman who "accidentally" uses my toothbrush every time she comes to visit.

Francesca (aka Cookie) and Mother Mary

But I was excited to try them. Would they give me superhuman hearing? I imagined I'd be able to use my newfound Spidey-sense to hear all sorts of things—a mouse in the house next door, or the dog tearing up the toilet paper in the bathroom.

Although the latter is a pretty safe bet, whether I hear it or not.

But when I put in the hearing aids, my heart sank. Not only did they feel weird and ticklish, they were clearly broken. The left one played irritating static, and the right one was completely dead, a very expensive plastic earplug. Meanwhile, my mom and I must have made Mother Mary put these hearing aids in ten times over her visit already, and all the while they were duds.

So we come to the final and most important rule, which is that grandmother whispering isn't about manipulation, it's about empathy. Sure, there are times when Mother Mary is sassy for sass's sake, but more often, she knows what she's talking about, and we'd do well to listen. You can't use tricks with a grandmother, you've got to use heart.

And when all else fails, throw the middle generation under the bus.

Feet Don't Fail Me Now

. . . .

By Lisa

Getting sick teaches many lessons.

And before I begin, let me say I know that having foot surgery isn't even being that sick, and certainly not as sick as many people. But it's what I'm working with now, and it taught me several lessons, which I'm about to inflict on you.

By the way, I also know that many of these lessons are not exactly news. But I did learn them for myself, and frankly, I think they bear repeating, especially if you've gotten used to living on your own, like me, or if you're just accustomed to being an adult, where you take care of yourself, your family, and the tristate area in general.

Or because you're a woman.

As the intake nurse said to me, "Your job is to lie still and let us take care of you. In other words, be a man."

Sorry, guys.

It may be a bad rap, but there it is.

And speaking for myself, I know that I hate to ask anybody for anything, much less help doing the basic things, like walking, dressing myself, or throwing up.

Generally I like to throw up on my own. But you haven't lived until you have a friend grab a wastebasket just in time.

We begin when I enter the hospital and relinquish all the

things I carry around, that I've come to think of as part of me: my clothes, purse, wallet, watch, and cell phone. On the plus side, I am given socks that are nicer than the ones I walked in with, because they match.

I wait to be processed, stripped down to what I really am: a human being with one extremely funky foot.

It's an odd sensation, being naked down to your genus.

Remember, I'm a bumper sticker of a woman. I wear my Phillies T-shirt to watch the game. At home.

Of course, our identity isn't any of our trappings, no matter how nice your watch, or how trendy your smartphone.

But you have to be smart to know that.

And then I meet a flock of nurses, each one asking me a set of questions pleasantly and carefully, as if they haven't asked them

Lisa preps for bunion surgery. Sexy outfit!

Lisa with besties Franca and Laura

ten thousand times before, and answering all my dumb questions with equal patience.

Let's hear it for nurses. I met a slew—Karen, Brigitte, Carol, and Mary Eileen, each one was nicer than the next.

I have never met a mean nurse. I have never even met an impatient nurse. Every nurse I meet, I want them to cuddle me, and one did. Nurses are funny, smart, kind, and impossibly hardworking and unsung.

Let's sing for nurses.

That was my first lesson.

And the other thing is that each nurse checked my ID bracelet for my birth date, and remarked that I looked younger than I am.

So nurses are really really great.

What did I learn?

That I look younger than I am.

Just kidding.

I learned that nurses aren't paid enough, because nobody could pay them enough to cuddle a middle-aged woman whose foot has its own on/off knob.

And the other thing I learned is how lucky I am in my girlfriends. They all know I hate to ask for help, so they all volunteered when I didn't ask, and they wouldn't take no for an answer. My girlfriend Laura moved in for the weekend, bringing Raisinets. My girlfriend Franca sent chocolate cake. My girlfriend Paula sent chocolate and pears.

You see the common thread.

Don't make me spell it out.

My girlfriend Nan stops by to make me dinner, and Mother Mary and Francesca call constantly to check on me, both begging to come and stay.

I say no. I'm fine now, and I don't need my daughter to take care of me just yet.

She'll have plenty of time to see me with a walker.

And Mother Mary's time for taking care of me is over.

She had the job for, like, fifty-seven years.

Slip Sliding Away

· · · · · · · · · · · · · · · · · ·

By Lisa

I used to make fun of plastic slipcovers, and now I wish I had them.

Please tell me you're old enough to know what plastic slip-covers are.

FYI, in the old days, people used plastic to preserve their furniture. Nowadays, people use plastic to preserve their faces.

No judgment here. Because I never thought I'd want plastic slipcovers, and now I do. The day could come when I want a plastic face.

You'll be the first to know. We'll both look surprised.

The Flying Scottolines weren't classy enough for plastic slipcovers. You don't need a plastic slipcover for a TV tray.

Now I'm grown-up, and I just got a new couch and chairs in a lovely floral fabric, but they're already blanketed with dog and cat hair. You would think I'd upholstered with fur.

I know this is my own fault. I could just forbid the dogs from getting on the furniture, but it's too late. You can't teach an old dog new tricks, and I can't be taught to keep the dogs off the furniture.

Of course, at the same time, I can't say I don't regret this de-cision. I've made mistakes in my life and have more than a few regrets, and sometimes I think that it was a mistake to let the dogs on the furniture.

I regret letting the dogs on the furniture every time I find dog hair on the back of my sweatpants, or on the side of my face when I nap on the couch. Even so, it's totally fun to snuggle on the couch with dogs. Peach is the Champion Cuddle Monster of all time, but she leaves behind white fur that has magnetic properties, attaching itself to all cushions in the tristate area.

And we're not even talking cat hair. Mimi and Vivi leave cat hair on the tops of the furniture, but cat hair can't be stopped, because cats can't be stopped.

Cat hair is not only magnetic, but weaves its way into the fibers of most clothing, in a process known only to cats and Satan.

If you have a cat, you have cat hair, and if you had plastic slipcovers, they'd be covered with cat hair, too.

So what I did in the family room was to buy three cheap coverlets and throw them over the new furniture, but then I spent all day looking at cheap coverlets and not my beautiful floral fabric. Hmm. But the quilts did the trick, because they got all dirty and hairy, so I couldn't take them off.

Still, what to do? This would be a suburban conundrum.

Then I thought of a third solution, which is my current one. I ordered three floral quilts online, which weren't that expensive, and now I look at them and pretend they're as nice as my new couch.

This isn't the best solution, either.

I had envisioned removing the quilts when I sat down or when people came over, but neither of these things happened. Whenever I sat down, I just moved the quilt over, so most of the time, I watch TV next to a pile of furry quilts, like a mound of hairy laundry.

And when people come over, I don't even bother moving the quilts, because it's too much trouble, unless the people were staying longer than half an hour or were someone I needed to impress.

Which would be nobody.

Most of the time, to avoid the hassle, I rushed people out, steering clear of the quilt-covered family room.

But now the quilts are covered with fur.

All of this sent me to the computer, there to find appliances known as the pet vac. Because marketing has convinced us that dog hair is different from other hairy schmutz and demands a different appliance. So long ago, I acquired an upright pet vac, but my upright pet vac can't be used on the furniture, so now I need something else.

Peach stretches out on Lisa's comfy chair.

Like what? A downright pet vac?

No, a hand pet vac.

For pet hands?

No, to use when I clean my flowery quilts. I looked online, and the bestselling pet vac is made by Dirt Devil.

Doubtless, in league with Satan.

In Which Spunky Teaches Me About Mother Mary

....

By Lisa

If you're worried about Spunky, you needn't be.

I got this.

And since I'm in a post-op life-lessons mood, I learned another one, this time from Spunky.

You may recall that Spunky is the orange tabby who belonged to my late friend Harry, who had rescued him as a kitten some fourteen years ago and lived alone with him all this time. I will remind you that Harry called himself Harry The Hermit, so you can guess that Spunky isn't exactly on Facebook.

Until the cat came to my house, about a month ago, he had never seen another cat, much less a dog or Ruby The Crazy Corgi, which is another creature entirely.

For this reason I had some trepidation about bringing Spunky home, but I loved Harry, and Harry loved Spunky, so it was natural to complete the circle of love. Also, I offer the best home any pet could have, because it's their world and I just pay for it.

Spunky's vet advised me to start Spunky out in his own room, but the thing about my house is that none of the rooms is closed off, especially to animals.

Like I said. Their world.

The only rooms with doors are the bedrooms, and Spunky couldn't be in mine, because all the dogs sleep with me, which left Daughter Francesca's bedroom.

Rather, Spunky's new bedroom.

My nest isn't empty, it contains a geriatric cat.

For the first day or two, he sat on the floor in a corner of his new bedroom, and he didn't respond to any attention, nor did he eat, drink, or poop. I was about to call the vet, but then poop appeared in his litter box and I rejoiced.

Yes, I have that much fun.

By the end of week one, Spunky was eating and drinking in his bedroom, but he never moved from under the desk, on top of the heater. I set up a little bed for him there, which he didn't use, and spent a little Spunky Time with him every day.

After the bunion surgery, it's easy to get down on the floor. The floor is my favorite place, because if I'm already there, I'm not falling there. I have yet to get the hang of the walker, which is as it should be. I don't plan on using one until never.

Though Spunky permitted himself to be petted, he neither purred nor recoiled. He was okay with my being there, but I didn't matter.

I felt the same way in my marriages.

But I'm not divorcing Spunky, though it would be cheaper.

Also on week one, I opened his door and put a gate in front of it, so he could come and go if he wished, or have a playdate with one of my other cats. But there was no sign of his coming out, nor of the other cats going in. I might have missed a secret nocturnal meeting, but I didn't install a cat cam. The day I spy on my pets, I need to get a life.

Or a midlife.

By the end of week two, there was no change in Spunky. Still every day I went in for Spunky Time and talked to him. I told him to join the family and have some fun, and finally, two days ago, he leaned into my hand to be petted.

Yay!

Later on, I have a conversation with Mother Mary. Of course, it's not about Spunky, because I still haven't told her about Harry's death. I'm still waiting for the right moment. In 2015.

"What are you up to?" I ask her, when she picks up.

"Laundry."

"Aw, why don't you go outside, to get some sun?"

"Nah."

"How about some shopping? Did you buy your new sheets?"

"Not yet. Maybe later."

I try to assess her tone. Is she depressed? Tired? Sick, negative? None of the above or all of the above? "Ma, you okay?"

"Sure, I'm fine," she says, chuckling. "How're you?"

And that's when it hits me.

She's Spunky.

She doesn't have to be doing anything—running errands, going places, making new friends. She's content, and at peace, just by being.

At her age, she's earned the right to be settled, and still.

And so has Spunky.

I went upstairs to tell him my revelation. I told Spunky he was home, where he could just relax, and that he had already joined the family, simply by being our elder statesman, who sits on the heater.

He looked up at me with round golden eyes, and he lifted his chin to be scratched.

No, he didn't purr.

He didn't have to.

Subtext

•••••••••••••••••

By Lisa

I'm loving texting, and I'll tell you why.

I need more stress in my life. I like my blood pounding in my veins, pressing against my arterial walls, transforming me into a walking pressure cooker.

Thank you, texting.

Let me take you back in time, friends.

I remember when there were things called letters, and in law school, I recall specifically waiting for a letter from a guy I had a crush on. We were dating, but he went away for the summer, and he never wrote. I actually checked the mail, every day. But no letters.

Face it, letters sucked.

But then, when I became a lawyer, the fax machine came along. To send a fax, we had to go down to the windowless bowels of the firm to a ring of hell called the Word Processing Department, which contained a highly underappreciated and undoubtedly underpaid group of women. None of the lawyers knew the names of the word processors, but I did because, like the firm's messengers, they were mostly Italian.

Yes, I did get my paycheck before everyone else. I had friends in low places.

Grazie.

Faxes used to be called facsimiles, and they came hot out of the machine, like you were baking at the office. We used to fax our lunch orders, which is the kind of thing that lawyers think is badass, and also I was dating somebody who used to send me poetry by fax. It didn't last until the advent of email, but I'm getting ahead of myself.

Computers came along, then the Internet, then email, which is now antique.

Back in the day, people would brag about how much email they got. Cool people got the most. By that time I had become an author, albeit a struggling one, and I heard from authors who got like fifty readers' emails a day.

I got no email except for spam, and back then, I even liked spam. This was before Viagra, which overstayed its welcome. By about three inches.

But soon we came to understand that email was just another task, and one that people expected you to perform right away, as in within a few hours or the same day.

We thought that fast.

How quaint.

Because then we got cell phones, iPhones, and BlackBerrys, and now we text like crazy and expect a reply in three, two, one . . .

NOW.

Texting is generational, but not always in ways you'd expect. For example, every time I'm with Daughter Francesca and she gets a text, I look over and ask her, "Aren't you going to get that?"

She'll shrug. "Whenever."

I blink. I can't ignore a text, like in the old days when I couldn't ignore a ringing phone.

What gives?

I went online, where I learned that every time somebody

reads a text, they get a surge of dopamine in the brain. You know about dopamine. It makes you dopey.

And its little burst of pleasure makes getting a text almost addictive, much like trolling the Internet in general. I can't explain why I am the one addicted to Francesca's texts when she isn't, except that I'm dopier.

And her iPhone, unlike my BlackBerry, actually beeps until you answer. My BlackBerry doesn't, maybe because it knows that uncool business types like me don't need to be told twice.

Yet Francesca just says no, and it took me a while before I realized that she was having ongoing text conversations with four different people throughout the day, all while we were running errands, making dinner, and cleaning up. To her credit, she did this with such finesse that I didn't notice, in contrast to my rookie reaching for my phone at each text alert, even during dinner.

Most of my texts are about work, some are about fun, but I mentally feel them piling up if I don't answer them. Texts are the new email, the never-ending list of Things To Do. I actually have a crack on the dry skin of my thumb from my Crack-Berry, and sometimes my neck hurts from looking down all the time.

"Mom," Francesca said. "You need to chill."

And I do, but I can't.

Except when it comes to dating, where the time you take to return the text is carefully measured, and examined. I wasn't sure of the protocol, but took a poll of my besties Laura and Franca, in addition to Francesca, and here's the skinny: If he replies right away, you reply right away. If he replies a day later, you reply a day later. In texting, symmetry rules.

Also it matters what you say and how you say it. I have edited my text messages more times than any of my novels. Francesca has coached me to be more informal and approving—ironically, the tone of every one of these columns, but nowhere in anything I text. Evidently, when you set up a date, "looking forward to it" isn't sexy.

And don't write xoxo before you have xoxoed.

Also, emoticons are out unless you're dating a twelve-year-old.

Bottom line, you have to keep your texts in context.

In-box of Letters

• • • • • • • • • • • • • • • • •

By Francesca

I was recently informed that I am at 95% capacity at my Gmail account.

Anyone who has a Gmail account will appreciate the irony. Gmail's tagline was once, "Why delete? Unlimited storage!" So for me to be at capacity feels like being told I'm walking too close to the edge of the world.

I'll be honest, I don't really understand the concept of physical space on the World Wide Web. I thought the Internet was like outer space—an infinite expanse of interconnected websites orbited by advertisements, black holes of discount shopping, and countless porn stars.

So if the Internet doesn't have physical space, how did I run out of it?

Well, I didn't exactly run out. Gmail tells me more storage exists, I just have to buy it.

Immaterial space doesn't come cheap.

So I set about trying to understand how I had exhausted my inexhaustible storage. I clicked to see the "oldest" email in my in-box and learn when I'd opened the account.

5/19/06 was my first email. It was from my then-boyfriend, who set up the account for me. The subject line was "test," and the body contained only one line, all lower case: "hey lovely lady."

Aw.

Well, I couldn't delete that.

I clicked through some of our lovey-dovey emails and found myself swooning all over again. Until I got a few pages further into the-honeymoon's-over stretch of emails, and I regained my senses.

Please, I can't afford any more airplane trips to get dumped.

But truthfully, I cried a little rereading our breakup emails. Viewing our year-plus relationship condensed within a few pages of messages, I could see that we really loved each other, we really tried, and it ended anyway. Two people with good hearts and the best intentions just couldn't make it work. I felt sad and comforted at the same time.

Despite the heartache, I wouldn't "Trash" any of it.

But I had to make room somewhere, so I got back to culling, this time starting with the insane number of emails between me and my best friend. Many were as short as one line, how important could they be?

Reading a few, I confirmed they weren't important.

They were hilarious.

I was crying again, this time with laughter. We had email threads riffing on boys, professors, classmates, celebrities, ourselves, everything.

I remember Harvard as a pressure cooker, but I'd forgotten how fantastic she and I were at letting off steam.

I started forwarding the best ones to her, but they were all the best ones, and soon I realized my email-blast-from-the-past was only going to clutter her in-box and mine.

Not helping.

The only person who emails me more than my best friend is

my mother. When I filter my in-box to show only those messages from lisa@scottoline.com, the system is so overwhelmed, it can't calculate an exact number, saying only that it's displaying one given page "of *many.*"

If you take this as proof that she's checking in on me all the time, you're mistaken.

She does that by phone.

My mom uses email to send me cell phone pictures of our pets. Our routine is that she sends the picture with no text at all, and I reply with a funny caption. It's like our own personal cuteoverload.com.

And "many" is polite. She has sent me hundreds—maybe thousands!—of them over the years, but her cell-phone-photography skills haven't improved one bit. Most of the pictures are blurry, marred by a finger, incredibly dark, or flashed so bright that the dog looks like Cujo.

Still, even the grainiest of images are cherished reminders of my furry family back home, and my in-box archive now includes photos of four pets that are no longer with us.

So I'm keeping them. Every last one.

I also tried eliminating old emails relating to schoolwork, but that task was a) arduous, because there was no common sender or keyword with which to fish for them, and b) anxiety-inducing, because rereading them returned me to that time when there was always too much to read, too many papers to write, and too harsh a curve on tomorrow's exam.

I could almost smell my all-nighter fuel of microwave popcorn and the sick-sweet taste of Red Bull.

Blech.

Word to the wise: Red Bull doesn't give you wings; it gives you the runs.

PTSD aside, since my hard-drive wipeout in the Great Crash of 2010, many of these emails contain the only remaining copies of papers I wrote for school—the first short story I wrote for a fiction workshop, even the three-page poem on *Beowulf* that I wrote in medieval verse.

I didn't say the stuff was cool.

They say nothing in this electronic age is permanent. I had many an English professor bemoan the lost art of letter writing, journaling, etc. But my in-box holds a more prolific record of my work, worries, laughs, and loves than I ever could've committed to paper. It doesn't offer a mere glimpse into my life at the time, it draws a map of my universe.

Looks like I'll be buying more storage.

Spoiled

•••••••••••••••••

By Lisa

Francesca and I love to go to the movies, though we disagree on everything about movie-going except the movie itself.

We generally love and hate the same movies, usually for the same reasons, and after the movie, we spend the evening deconstructing the plot and analyzing what worked and what didn't and why, which might be an occupational hazard.

But that's where our agreement ends.

Our differences begin before we even leave the house, because I like to go early to arrive at the theater at least forty-five minutes before the show. I hate to miss the beginning of the movie, even nowadays, when the movie doesn't begin until after the previews, Coke commercials, local Realtor commercials, cell phone and texting warnings, then the little man driving a go-kart on a filmstrip.

Francesca thinks we should miss all of this, and of course, she is clearly right. But she indulges me, which is what filial duty is all about. Moms are entitled to be humored from time to time, as payback for all the little-kid rainbow drawings we said were great.

Please. How hard is it to draw a rainbow, anyway? Open any

old-school Crayola box, and get busy. Red, orange, yellow, green, blue, purple. We get it.

Plus they owe us for labor, too. I mean, really. And I had *back* labor. As far as I'm concerned, that child should go when and where I say, forever.

Anyway at the candy counter, we continue to disagree, though I don't concede I'm wrong so easily. I like to get a Diet Coke, a small popcorn, and Raisinets, and eat it all myself. She likes to get a bigger popcorn and share.

She knows I will not share my Raisinets. Half the reason I go to the movies is for the Raisinets.

I don't like to share because I'm a fifty-six-year-old woman, and as such, have spent a lifetime sharing. Now I want it all for myself. It's my turn, and my popcorn.

So I coerce Francesca into getting her own goodies, and we enter the theater, where we disagree over the seating. I like to sit close, in the front third of the theater. Francesca likes the back third. You might think that the easiest thing to do would be to compromise on the middle third, but that doesn't solve the problem.

Why?

Because then we divide the middle third into thirds, and she wants to sit in the back third and I want to sit at the front third. We could further compromise by sitting in the middle third, but the seats there are full of mothers and daughters who compromise more quickly than we do.

Also I like to sit near the end of the row, as I have to get up at least once to go to the bathroom, not only because I'm middle-aged, but because I wouldn't share my Diet Coke. She likes to sit in the middle, because she is twenty-five years old and pees once a day, like most camels.

We don't compromise on this, and usually take what seats we

can get. I cope by not feeling embarrassed about having to go to the bathroom when nobody else does. The old bat climbing over your shoes on the way out of the row is me, poster child for urinary incontinence.

But these are mere quibbles. Our biggest disagreement is over spoilers.

I love spoilers.

I love to know the ending of a movie before I go. I read every review I can and every spoiler alert. A spoiler alert doesn't spoil anything for me.

In fact, I don't go to a movie unless I know the ending. I'm a suspense writer who doesn't like to be in suspense.

This issue came up recently, with Steven Spielberg's *War Horse*. As soon as the movie came out, Francesca knew it was right up our alley, and I did, too. But the previews made clear that it was a story about a boy who lets his beloved horse go to war, and I wasn't going to the movie unless I knew he got the horse back.

And not a different horse.

And not the horse's baby, like they do in every animal movie ever.

Guaranteed in the movies that if they kill off the animal you love, there will be a new litter of whatever by the final credits.

That doesn't wash with me.

I love what I love, and I want it back.

Things die in real life. If they don't, that's entertainment.

And if I'm holding popcorn, I want entertainment.

I'm divorced twice, remember? I require a happy ending.

So I wasn't going to see *War Horse* unless I knew the horse got home, but Francesca absolutely didn't want to know the ending. She never wants to know the ending. She covers spoiler alerts with her hand.

Who raised this child?

I asked everyone I knew if the horse got back, but no one knew, because the movie had just opened and it was Christmas. Francesca wanted to go, but I refused, and I said we had to wait until I could find out the ending.

"Don't find out the ending," she said, unhappily.

"Why not? I won't tell you."

"I'll know. Because if you find out the ending and still want to go, I'll know that the horse comes back."

Hmm. She had me there.

For a moment.

Then I did what any good mother would do. I lied to my daughter.

I found out the ending, but told her I didn't.

And now I can't tell you if we went to the movie or not, because then you'll know the ending.

The End.

To Everything, There Is a Season

. . . .

By Lisa

At this point, I'm a brain in a jar.

Here's what I mean. We know I had the bunion surgery, and I can't put any weight on my right foot. I'm supposed to stay off my feet for the next seven weeks, and luckily, I'm one of the few people in the world whose job requires them to stay off their feet.

And apply my butt to a chair, my fingers to a laptop, and write.

So I thought the whole surgery thing would be easy, and I was wrong.

It's paradise.

At least now, because I've surrendered. I get it now, though I was skeptical at first. I didn't really believe that you had to stay off your feet all that time, because I never follow directions, in general. Usually I don't even read them. I used to think this was fun and rebellious of me, but now I think I was just stupid.

Because by the end of the first week after surgery, I had fallen twice.

The first time I fell was when I was trying to lift my golden Penny onto the bed, and the second was the next day, when I woke up in the middle of the night because Peach had jumped off the bed, and I forgot I'd had foot surgery and took a step without my walker.

Dogs, beds, and a bunionectomy are the disaster trifecta.

And the pain from both falls was considerable, which is a stoic way of saying OOOOOOWWWWWWWWWWW WWWWWWWWW!

So now I see the light.

I got religion.

After the fall(s).

And I remembered that my wonderful doctor had said that the only time he had to reoperate on someone was on a woman who had fallen. Of course, when he told me that, I thought, What a klutz she must have been!

And now I'm the klutz.

Lesson learned.

Shut up and heal.

So I sit upstairs in my bedroom, waiting for a bone that has been sawed apart to grow back together, like the anatomical equivalent of watching paint dry.

Being still isn't something that comes naturally to me, because I keep feeling the urge to *do* things to heal. Doing things makes sense, and not doing things feels odd.

And lazy.

Plus, I feel so guilty that people have to tote food to me and take it away, walk the dogs for me, let in the UPS guy, and do all the normal things for me, that people do for themselves.

Turns out there's nothing you can do to heal except, be still.

Sit still.

Lie still.

Healing is doing nothing.

So I sit still and write, which is the brain-in-a-jar part.

I do little things, though I don't know if they help. For

example, I started taking calcium citrate twice a day, because I heard that it grows bone, and I wanted to heal faster.

Grow, bone, grow!

Come to think of it, healing faster may be more wrong thinking. Our greeting cards say Get Well Soon and Speedy Recovery, but my guess is that no proper recovery is speedy.

Sports cars should be speedy. Recoveries, slow as tar.

Even the Bible says that there should be a time to heal, just as surely as there is a time to go to the dry cleaners, a time to do the laundry, and a time to empty the dishwasher.

I'm quoting the newest translation.

All the purposes under heaven have their time, and the way we usually multitask, those times are all at once.

But no longer.

Not for me.

I just saw an article in today's paper saying that stillness and solitude lead to greater creativity.

Good news for single gals with a bum foot.

I'm already working on my next book.

A Time to Heal.

Hang-Ups

. . . .

By Francesca

Last night I hung up the phone on my mother.

That sounds harsh, but you should know I employed our modified hang-up, the one we use when we're angry but have the presence of mind to keep some perspective. It goes something like this:

"Ugh! I'm hanging up, but I love you," I say in the span of one second, so it sounds like, "ImhangingupbutIloveyou."

Click.

My mom trained me to do this at a young age. If we were arguing and I tried to storm out, she'd remind me that one of us COULD DIE AT ANY MOMENT, so the last words we say to each other should be, "I love you."

In Italian, the word for love is *guilt.*

I'm not proud of hanging up on my mother, I apologized later, but it happens. Every mother-daughter relationship has logged some hang-ups on phone record. It's not the most enlightened behavior, but when an argument gets out of control, it's better to end the conversation before it gets uglier. But you still want to get the last word.

Who am I, Mother Teresa?

Even she was Daughter Teresa at some point.

When you're a teenager, you can slam the door. Well, I

couldn't, because we had dogs. And if you close a door to a dog, whatever's on the other side of it becomes the most interesting thing in the world. So two minutes after my dramatic you-may-never-see-me-again door slam, I'd have to open it to let our golden, Lucy, in.

Golden retrievers are the family therapists of the canine world.

But after you grow up and move out, you mature past slamming doors.

And hang up the phone instead.

My mom and I have elevated it to an art form. Our technique is so advanced, we have categories of hang-ups.

There's the enigmatic Fake Hang-Up. The Fake Hang-Up comes from one of our favorite movies, the Bill Murray comedy *What About Bob?* In the film, Murray's character, Bob, is so incapable of believing that his therapist would set a limit on him and end a call, he blithely asks, "Is this a fake hang-up? It's a fake hang-up!"

That movie came out twenty-one years ago, but that line is still so funny to us that if one of us stays quiet on the phone for more than two seconds, the other will say, "Is this a fake hang-up?"

Normally this is good for a laugh, but the mere existence of the Fake Hang-Up takes the wind out of all future I'm-actually-really-angry hang-ups.

Maybe that's a good thing.

But not all of our hang-ups are angry. The Commercial Break Hang-Up is the gentlest of all because it's mutual; my mom and I both hang up on each other at the same time.

This hang-up has a history. When I was growing up, every night I would climb into my mom's bed with her and the dogs and watch the late-night talk shows. Now I'm old enough to have the TV in my bedroom, but too old to live with my mom. Luckily, we've found a way to restore the tradition.

Whenever the guest is a particular favorite of ours, we call each other and watch together over the phone. That way, when Sarah Jessica Parker walks out, we can gush over her outfit in real time. Or if Hugh Jackman is on, we can discuss how the real reason we like him is because he's a family man, and not because he's gorgeous, tall, has washboard abs, *that accent,* or the adorable way his face crinkles when he smiles.

Sigh.

But our simulcast never works for long, because for some inexplicable reason our televisions never sync up. Both of us watch NBC in HD on the East Coast, and yet I can hear a half-second delay on my mom's television, creating an annoying echo for both of us. Why is her identical channel slower than mine?

Maybe everything sounds slower and wrong-er when it's coming from your mother.

So now we yap away during the commercials, then hang up on each other the instant the show returns, with not much more than an, "Ooh, show's back on—"

Click.

Granted, it's always a little insensitive to hang up on your family members, but this act comes from a place of love.

For quality television.

Sometimes my mom and I are blameless, as with the Dogfight Hang-Up. My mom and I will be enjoying a peaceful conversation, when all of a sudden I hear Tasmanian devils growling on the other end, my mom yells out, and the call drops. It's dramatic until you've heard it the hundredth time. I usually give Mom a few minutes to get the whip and the chair, then I'll call her back to make sure everything is okay.

Considering my mother's history with dogfights, I can't be sure she'll have a finger left to dial with.

Why all the hang-ups? I'm supposed to be more mature than this, I'm twenty-five years old and my mom is, well, also mature.

Maybe because most of the time we can't stop talking to each other. She'll call me "just to say good night," and we'll end up chatting for half an hour. Our calls never end with a simple goodbye. It's usually a stutter-step of "Bye—oh, but I was meaning to tell you . . ." or "I have to get back to work, but before I forget . . ." There's always one more funny story I want to tell her or one last worry only she can soothe.

It's hard to say goodbye.

Sometimes it's easier to just hang up.

Nobody's Passenger

. . . .

By Lisa

I have often said that there are many pleasures to being single, and among them is that you get to be in the driver's seat.

I mean this literally. In other words, I'm not talking about the road of life. I'm talking about I-95.

Not all of these columns are metaphorical. Sometimes a train is just a train.

But a cigar is always a phallic symbol.

I've been single for a long time now, and I'm used to driving myself everywhere. And I love every minute of myself as a driver. I'm a good and careful driver. I go slow and pay attention. I look around all the time. I watch out for the other guy. I scan his hands for a wedding band.

Just kidding.

I never got to drive myself when I was married, and I hated that. Why?

Frankly, because I never really liked the way that men drive.

Or maybe it was just my men, but it started with my late father.

Let me say for the record that I adored my father. He was a great guy, calm and easygoing, except when he was behind the wheel. Then he didn't become angry, but he liked to go fast. Not crazy fast, but well over the speed limit.

And this in the olden days, when the speed limit was 65.

You may be too young to remember those days. Back then, the retirement age was also 65, but times have changed. Nowadays the speed limit is 55, and the retirement age is 235.

Which means that there are plenty of eighty-five-year-olds driving themselves to the office at 82 mph.

Not a good combo.

Anyway, even when my father drove at the speed limit, he sped to the traffic light, then stopped short, over and over and over, so the ride would be herky-jerky and ultimately nauseating. You could get carsick with my dad, even in the front seat. It drove my mother nuts, and after they divorced, it drove my stepmother nuts.

Divorce doesn't solve everything.

Just in my case.

We all nagged my father about his driving, and he tried to comply, but it didn't last. He wasn't passive-aggressive, but he was forgetful. He'd try to toe the line, but sooner or later, he'd go back to his old habits.

Like me and chocolate cake, when I'm on a diet.

It's only a matter of time before we're reunited.

And it feels so good.

Anyway, I think the way that my father drove is the way that all men drive, because every man I've ever driven with drives the same way. Thing One, Thing Two, and all the other things.

Evidently, a car is a phallic symbol, too.

Okay, I won't speculate as to whether this habit is genital, or congenital.

And as far as driving goes, it's not that I'm a control freak. I just like to go slow, and enjoy the ride. I sing, I listen to audiobooks, and I think, or talk to myself.

Yes, I'm that crazy lady in the car next to you. I act like I'm talking on a hands-free phone, but I'm talking to myself.

Maybe Ruby can drive next time.

And I don't think I'm alone.

I have figured out this much: Men drive to get somewhere, and women enjoy the process more.

And because men are so concerned with Point A to Point B, they drive too fast. They don't leave enough space between cars. They switch lanes too often. They pass all the time.

And they never, *ever* use blinkers.

It's not that men expect you to read their minds.

Women expect you to read their minds.

Men expect you to deal.

I was reminded of this again after my bunion surgery, when I had to ask a male friend of mine to drive me to the foot doctor. My friend is a great guy, calm and mellow like my father, but when he drove us, we zoomed and stopped, zoomed and stopped, the whole trip, and I got up close and personal with way too many bumper stickers.

IF YOU CAN READ THIS, YOU'RE TOO CLOSE.

And we were.

Not even a podiatrist can cure a lead foot.

Look, I know that men take more risks in life, and that's a good thing. Steve Jobs, Bill Gates, and even Christopher Columbus all took great risks and reaped great rewards.

But what about that guy who married and divorced Kim Kardashian in seventy-two days, whatever his name was.

Shoulda driven slower, if you ask me.

I myself wait until I mail my thank-you notes to file my divorce papers.

If it's the road of love, I want it to last forever.

All We Have to Do Is Take This Lie and Make It True

. . . .

By Lisa

I just lost five pounds. As they say, Ask me how!

The answer is, Denial.

Not that I didn't really lose the weight, but I lost it by going into denial.

Denial is something I'm really good at. All of the Flying Scottolines are denial experts.

Denial is in our DNA.

In fact, we think DNA stands for Do Not Acknowledge.

Our exciting family history is replete with examples. For example, none of us realized that Brother Frank was gay even though he never dated a woman, had a long-term guy "friend," and was never without a tank top.

Of mesh.

And when Frank and his "friend" moved in together, they shared a bedroom and both bought bulldogs.

Still, we missed that obvious clue.

If you see matching dogs, look for a gay couple.

And when Frank got a job as a bartender in a gay bar, we figured it was the only job he could get. And when he finally told us, we still didn't believe it, and when we finally did and told other people, they all knew.

Bottom line, it didn't matter to my mother or father that Frank was gay, plus we were happy for the extra dog.

I have top-quality, Grade-A denial, and it's finally working in my favor.

Here's what happened.

You may recall that I have high cholesterol, and I was going to see the doctor, so I needed a blood test. And it had to be a fasting blood test, which means that you can't eat anything after seven o'clock at night.

Uh-oh.

I have a hobby, which is eating after seven o'clock at night.

I actually look forward to seven o'clock, so I can start eating, especially in winter. Some people like winter white, but I like winter weight.

Who needs a Snuggie when you *are* a Snuggie?

I finish dinner and then start eating, so everything I eat after seven o'clock has a name.

Dessert.

But I knew I had a blood test, and I never cheated on a test before and wasn't about to start. So I vowed not to eat after seven o'clock, and the way I accomplished this was by eating up to-but-not-including seven o'clock, then going upstairs and watching TV.

I knew I had to put some distance between the refrigerator and me. The first floor ain't big enough for the both of us.

So I stayed upstairs and came down only to walk the dogs at eleven o'clock, and even then I passed the refrigerator with gritted teeth.

So far, so good.

But to make a long story short, the next morning, I got an important phone call and I couldn't get to the lab, so I decided to postpone the blood test until the next day. And when the next night rolled around, I didn't eat after seven o'clock, using the same method, for the second night in row.

And succeeded!

Then something else happened, merely by accident, or as proof of a God who watches over middle-aged women with middles.

My bunion surgery got scheduled and I had to hurry up and get another blood test, and so I didn't eat after seven o'clock, for the third night in a row.

And when I got on the scale the next day, I had lost a whole entire pound.

WOW!

And suddenly, I decided to get a new hobby.

Because I realized, if I had a blood test every day, I might be able to lose more weight. But of course, I didn't need to have a real blood test, if I could convince myself that I had an imaginary blood test.

So that's what I did.

And it worked!

And then I had the bunion surgery and had to stay upstairs, and could only eat when kind souls brought me food, and one week later, I lost five pounds!

It may not sound like a lot, but to me, it's a miracle. And I hope to lose more, on my patented Denial Diet.

Not that I think you can try this at home. You of healthy mind may not be able to convince yourself of a lie the way I can.

After all, I convinced myself that nobody notices the dog-hair tumbleweeds in the corners of my house.

I also convinced myself that the occasional turd in my fireplace is from a passing goose, and not from the cats, telling me to change the litter box.

Going back, I had even convinced myself I had a happy marriage.

Twice.

And going forward, I have convinced myself that someday, I will find true love with a man.

Who doesn't wear a tank top.

Hey, it could happen.

Called to Order

•••••••••••••••

By Lisa

I didn't sleep last night, because I was at a board meeting.

It was held in my bed, by myself, except for four dogs, who took notes.

Here's what I mean.

Little Tony decided he had to go to the bathroom at three in the morning, which meant I had to take him out, and long story short, I couldn't go back to sleep, so I decided it was time for a Board meeting.

This is something I do sometimes, but not every quarter. The Scottoline Board meets whenever I can't sleep, which is rare. I sleep like a baby, because I'm old and tired. My problem isn't sleeping, it's staying awake.

But the Board meeting is a good thing, because it's how I figure out what I'm doing in my life. In other words, it's my Board of Life, but not my Bored of Life.

Quite the contrary.

I feel lucky and have a great life, but it's a busy time to be alive, for all of us. And I've found that it really helps me to set aside some quiet time and think about all the facets of my life, so that I can run it better.

God knows when I started doing this, but it was when I

remembered how we used to say we were "leading" our lives, and I realized I was living a life, but not leading one.

I wasn't running anything, and that was leaving me vulnerable to being run. I had no agenda, and I learned that if you don't have an agenda, someone will have one for you. And it will be what they want, not what you want.

Remember, nature abhors a vacuum.

I abhor a vacuum cleaner.

Plus my happy-go-lucky life without agenda resulted in some really bad marriages, I mean, er, decisions.

So I realized that leading my life takes conscious effort and planning, and maybe some corporate overlay, but without the 401k.

This is where you find out that I'm crazy.

So what I do is picture a long, glistening mahogany board table, with me at the head.

Because I'm the boss.

I may not be the boss of you, but I'm the boss of me. Come to think of it, the Me Company isn't a democracy, so really I'm Queen of Me.

For Life.

By the way, I did incorporate last year, when I named my company Smart Blonde, LLC., which is false advertising.

None of us blondes is dumb.

We're not even really blond.

Anyway, then I visualize five women sitting around the conference table, and each is Head of her Department, of which there are five:

Family, Home, Work, Money, and Carbohydrates.

Obviously, in order of importance.

Next, each Department Head gives me a progress report, in order. For example, the head of the Family Department tells me that Francesca is doing fine, but doesn't know if Mother Mary got her upright MRI.

Hmm.

I task her with calling Mother Mary, and I make a note in my BlackBerry, since I'm not sure imaginary board members own PDAs and I'm not taking any chances.

That's the kind of monarch I am.

Next, the Head of the Home Department reports that we might need a TV in my office, since the old one stopped working two weeks ago and I'm paying for a cable box with no TV.

I consider this carefully because, between us, the Head of the Home Department spends money like crazy. She wants everything—new rugs, new sheets, more curtains, and a nicer comforter. She even wants a mudroom. The more money I give her, the more she spends.

I suspect she may have a substance-abuse problem.

The substance is chintz.

So I turn, metaphorically speaking, to the Head of the Money Department and ask her if we can afford a new TV. By the way, the Head of the Money Department is the only Department Head who isn't me.

She's Maria Bartiromo.

Nobody would trust me with my money.

Maria reminds me that we have rewards points burning a hole in our collective pocket and we can get a small TV, for free. I task the Head of the Home Department with ordering a TV, but she seems disappointed. She still wants that mud-room.

Told you.

I listen to the other reports, make notes, and end up with the Head of the Carbohydrates Department.

She doesn't think we needed that extra piece of toast at breakfast.

What a bitch.

So I fire her.

It's good to be Queen.

I Am Mother Mary

•••••••••••••••••

By Lisa

Everybody says you'll turn into your mother someday, but I already have.

I realized this happened when I got a new computer. I've been a longtime PC person, though we're meant to feel uncool by Apple ads.

Ask me if I care.

One of the many advantages of getting older is that you care less about what people think of you, or what's cool. I'll tell you what's cool:

Elastic waistbands.

Right? Show of hands.

Come on, even teenagers like elastic waistbands. Most of the time, they're wearing sweatpants with drawstrings. But drawstrings are for the young. Why?

They pee once a day.

You know I'm telling the truth.

Daughter Francesca is like a camel. Whenever we're together, I'm in the bathroom ten times a day, to her one.

This may be an overshare, but why stop now?

Drawstrings are no friend to the middle-aged woman. If I had a drawstring, I'd be tying bows all day long, like I was wrapping Christmas presents.

I write for a living, so my PC contained eleven novels, three hundred columns, various book reviews, and all of my reader email, including ads for cheap Viagra. I must get ten of these emails a day, and they evade my spam filter with deceptive subject lines like, "Lisa, here's the answer to that question you asked." Or "Lisa, should we finalize that meeting?"

This makes me laugh. I'm at the point where if you use my first name, I ignore your email.

Ironic, no?

Also, it's baffling that whatever evil genius sends these emails doesn't realize that anybody with the name Lisa isn't going to be the one buying the Viagra.

I have a vagina, people.

Maybe they can't spell.

Though I suppose there are women who do the Viagra shopping for their men, in the same way that some women buy the condoms, but if you ask me, that's one step too far.

Ladies, if you're buying the Viagra, you're not only wearing the pants in the family, you're filling them.

But left alone, women will overfunction, God bless us. I guess it's like buying a birthday card for your mother-in-law, and you really really really like your mother-in-law.

If you follow.

My computer had been sending me messages telling me I was running out of disc space, which at my age, usually means you're having a lower back problem. But this time, it meant my computer was full, and I'd already upgraded its memory twice.

I know what you're thinking. If we could upgrade our memory, we'd be in good shape.

Bottom line, I had to buy a new computer and I found myself in an Apple store, considering one. Francesca loves hers, and said it was easier to use. And that got my attention.

Easier is my middle name.

Easier is the lure of elastic waistbands, after all, so I started viewing Apple as the elastic waistband of computers.

And I got one.

It's easier in some ways, but not in others. The good news is that it was easy to get started, because all you have to do is plug it in, and amazingly, it has no tower to put under the table, so it looks pretty in the family room.

Still I miss my END key, which took me instantly to the end of the sentence, and I can't get used to not having a DELETE key.

Why did they delete the DELETE key?

I wish there were more DELETE keys in the world. In fact, I wish life had a DELETE key. But I guess it does, and it's called Divorce.

Anyway, I started to work on my new computer, and all of a sudden, the way I used to do things is no more. I have to change everything, and I'm cranky.

It was about this same time that I called Mother Mary, to say hello. I asked her, "How are you, Ma?"

"Terrible," she answered. "I'm mad at your brother."

"Why? More tattoos?"

"No. He bought me the little bottles of beer instead of the big ones I like."

She's not an alcoholic, she just likes a Bud Lite at night. And she leaves half of the bottle, so I know what my brother was thinking. "You don't like the little ones?"

"No, I need the big ones."

"Why?"

"To belch."

Yes, this is my family. Impressed yet? "Maybe you can get used to the little ones."

"No, I can't belch with the little ones. I need the big ones back."

"Change is good, Ma," I said, eyeing my new computer.

"Change sucks," said Mother Mary.

Or maybe I said that.

Does it matter?

We're the same person, after all.

Get Well, or Else

• • • • • • • • • • • • • • • •

By Francesca

I have a nasty spring cold. I sneeze over my soup, burn my tongue on hot tea, and shuffle around after the dog, who manages to shred every tissue in my apartment.

Yesterday, I braved the outside world—or considering the way I look when I'm sick, the outside world braved me—to get some pharmacy provisions: cold medicine, throat lozenges, more Kleenex for the dog to destroy, tabloid magazines.

Trashy magazines are chicken soup for the brain.

Once home, I retrieved my favorite honey-lemon Halls cough drops from the shopping bag. As I began to unwrap one, I saw there were phrases written all over the wrapper, lines like:

"Don't try harder. Do harder!"

"March forward!"

"Impress yourself today!"

"The show must go on. Or work."

I rubbed my watery eyes to make sure I was reading it right. Was my cough drop yelling at me? I thought I was hallucinating. That was until I saw, written in all caps in the corner:

"A PEP TALK IN EVERY DROP™."

Oh yeah, trademark that sucker. That's your golden goose, right there.

Could there be a product less suited to tough love than a cough drop?

Hey, Halls, I'm sick. It hurts to swallow. I'm so desperate, I've turned to your disgusting medicated candy for comfort. Cut me some slack, will ya?

I'll "Take charge and mean it!" a different day.

I get what they were going for, I guess. Trying to motivate me to "Get through it," as one of the less accusatory phrases said. But listen, there's a difference between cheerleading and brow-beating.

Where is the empathy? Why not print useful, motherly advice like, "Get some rest" or "Drink fluids"? How about "You'll feel better in the morning," or even good ol' "Get Well Soon"? Sometimes you need a gentle touch, cough drops.

I suppose subtlety is a lot to ask from a lozenge you can smell on someone's breath from across the room.

I tried to think of the last time my food had something to say, and I was reminded of my favorite part of Chinese takeout—the fortune cookies. I love them so much, I don't even mind when they throw in three on the assumption that, surely, this quantity of dumplings, lo mein, and tofu with broccoli must be intended for an entire family, not just a single woman.

Hey, I'm still growing.

Point is, fortune cookies have the right idea. They might offer an intriguing forecast: "A pleasant surprise is waiting for you."

It's always pleasant. Doom is bad for digestion.

Or an insight into your character: "You love Chinese food."

Scarily accurate!

A motivational maxim: "A person is never to [sic] old to learn."

A refresher on grammar *and* irony!

A revelation from your personal life: "Your ex-boyfriend totally misses you."

Okay, so I never got that one. But he'd better.

In a way, all carbs tell my future:

Guilt.

Incorporating writing into food can be smart marketing. Diet be darned, I justify buying these certain chocolate bars based on their cute gimmick: The brand is called "Chocolove," and every bar comes with a romantic poem printed inside the wrapper.

Isn't that the sweetest idea? No English major can resist it.

Not that I've ever read the poem. By the time I tear into the wrapper, I've completely forgotten there was a literary component to my purchase. I'm too preoccupied with the rich, delicious, dark chocolate about to hit my taste buds.

Oh well. It's the thought that counts.

If the treadmill had love poems and compliments written on it, I might be more inclined to run on it.

So, Halls, I reject your "PEP TALK IN EVERY DROP™," and I suggest you reconsider your marketing campaign. You catch more bees with honey than with menthol. I'm taking a stand for the right of sick people to feel sorry for themselves.

Unfortunately, righteous indignation is not a cold remedy. I didn't want to admit defeat, but my throat was still sore. I swallowed. It hurt. I had no choice.

I put the cough drop in my mouth.

It tasted bitter.

Gadget Girl

....

By Lisa

The salesman told me a snowblower would change my life,
but so far it hasn't.

What a snow job.

Because it only snowed once thus far, for two whole inches.
I'm not complaining, but that snowfall cost me $300 an inch.

I didn't even use the damn thing, because I'm still not
walking after bunion surgery, so I had to pay someone to
shovel, and he didn't think there was enough snow to use the
snowblower.

Make that $350 an inch.

You may recall, I thought about buying a snowblower after
six impossible winters, then finally broke down and bought one
a few months ago, and have evidently saved all of us from another impossible winter. If I buy an umbrella, it will never rain
on any of us, ever.

I guess it's unfair to blame the weather on a snowblower, but
I do regret having bought it, at least so far. Should I wish for
snowstorms?

Or write John Deere a Dear John letter?

I love gadgets, but my record with them is hit-or-miss. There
is no in between. Either the gadget is great or it sucks, and I have
succumbed to the siren song of many a sucky gadget.

I'm talking about you, bamboo steamer.

Turns out you can steam anything in a normal stainless-steel pot, with an inch of water and a lid. But only a bamboo steamer will retain water, so that it grows attractive mold.

In case you want to steam penicillin.

I'm also talking to you, costly wooden chopping board, which warps and comes apart at the seams. I am such a sucker that I even bought the Mystery Oil they sell you to keep it clean.

No joke, it's actually called Mystery Oil.

I may have nobody but myself to blame for that one. You'll be happy to know I passed up the snake oil.

I don't have any snakes.

By the way, in my view, a wooden chopping block qualifies as a gadget. Admittedly, I'm not being overly technical about definitions, especially when it comes to things I waste money on.

Snowfall before Lisa bought a snowblower

Lisa finally breaks down and buys a shiny new snowblower.

My kitchen is otherwise full of gadgets I bought on impulse, or was given as wedding gifts in my ex-life. Yes, after my divorces, I kept the juicer and waffle iron.

Because I got squeezed and burnt.

Then there are gadgets that are aspirational. I want to be the kind of woman who makes her own pasta, so I bought a pasta machine.

I have never used it.

Because I'm not that kind of woman.

Mother Mary used it to make homemade pasta, and she showed Francesca how while I watched them, sipping a gin and tonic.

Cooking is fun!

Also I bought a pizzelle maker, for the same reason. I'm

The amount of snow that has fallen since Lisa bought the snowblower

caught up in some Old World Italian fantasy. Some woman dream of being Martha Stewart, I dream of being Anna Magnani.

You might need to Google that, if you're under seventy years old.

Next time this mood strikes, I'm going to Olive Garden.

Once I even tried to make my own wine, which caused me to buy a gadget with a curly glass tube that you stick in this huge glass jug filled with crushed wine goop that I drove two hours to buy.

I did not crush the grapes with my own feet. I'm Anna Magnani, not Lucille Ball.

I set the huge jug on the kitchen counter, where it was supposed to ferment, for three years.

I'm not kidding. I commit.

But all it did was scent the kitchen with vinegar, then morph into purple tar.

Francis Ford Coppola I'm not.

And John Deere I'm not, either.

Maybe I'm Inspector Gadget?

Jazz Hands

• • • • • • • • • • • • • • • •

By Lisa

Here's how I feel about aging gracefully.

It's overrated.

Also I don't know what it means. If it means getting older without whining, count me out.

You can always whine. You can whine about your wrinkles, your hips, or your cholesterol levels. You can whine about anything you want to, and don't let anyone tell you different.

You have to fight for your right to whine.

But if it means getting older while trying not to, you can also count me out. I know a losing cause when I see one.

I'm divorced twice, remember?

You can't stop getting older, unless you die. If you think about it that way, getting older isn't a losing cause, it's a winning cause.

Let's all get older. Yay!

If getting older is inevitable, so is looking older. You can't stop either process. You might be able to Botox it and fill it and stuff it for a while, but not forever. Trying not to look older is like trying to cover the sky with your hands.

And sometimes the changes as we get older, and look older, can be remarkable and even sort of beautiful.

In fact, our hands are a case in point.

I say this because, the other day, I picked up my car keys and happened to notice that my hand was looking really old. It was dry and kind of crepey, and the back of it was covered with faint brown flecks.

Age spots.

Or as I think of them, constellations.

If you connect them, they form George Clooney.

Really, why waste time with Orion? Does he have a house in Italy?

No, all he has is a belt. And I don't want to fight with a man, over accessories.

I didn't even recognize my own hand. It didn't look like it belonged to me, though it was sticking out of my coat sleeve. It wasn't the way I remembered it, when it was young.

And hot.

When you know something well, they say you know it like the back of your hand, but I didn't know the back of my own hand. I called Daughter Francesca and told her as much, and she laughed.

She said, "I was just thinking that myself. I noticed I have Mom Hands."

I smiled. "What?"

"I looked at my hands, and the veins are getting bigger, either because I'm working out or getting older, and they reminded me of your hands."

"And you threw up?"

"No, not at all. I like it. I always loved your hands."

Which made me think.

I always loved Mother Mary's hands, too. I remember everything about them, even as she aged. I know my mother's hands like the back of my hand.

Only better.

Her fingers were little, and the nails had a neat curve, and when I was younger, she polished them with hot corals and frosted whites, the colors of the sixties, if you were a secretary.

And not a hippie.

I'm betting that I'm not the only one who can summon up an image of their mother's hands.

How about it? Try it now. Show of hands.

And way back when, she wore a thick gold wedding ring, a basketweave pattern that had a warm and lovely hue. I used to try on her wedding ring, sliding it up and down my finger, taking it off and on.

I think they call that foreshadowing.

And as her hands aged, I didn't love them any less. Just as I didn't love her any less.

No one of us loves anyone less, simply because they age.

How they look is beside the point.

I imagine this is what men are always trying to tell women when we fret about our wrinkles. The way we look doesn't matter to someone we love, so why does it matter to us?

And now, when I think about hands, I think about what they do. Mother Mary's hands cooked, typed, and hugged us. And they pinched like, well, a mother.

My hands can't type, but they hunt and peck. And they hug, pat, and scratch a cat behind the ears.

And applaud.

They can always find a tick on a dog, but not always a key on a BlackBerry.

Guess which is more important, to me.

You can tell a lot about a person by their hands, especially as they age. We all get the face we deserve, but we earn our hands.

We become handy.

And I'm proud of that.

You should be, too.

An Open Letter from an Open Heart

. . . .

By Lisa and Francesca

By now you know that Francesca and I talk all the time about everything, whether it's carbohydrate counts, hair, men, dogs, or a new recipe for salmon. We end each conversation with "I love you" or "have fun," probably because it's our general wish for each other that we are happy. Most parents, when asked, would say that what they want most is for their kids to be happy.

But for this last chapter, we wanted to go beyond "be happy." We wanted to share our true wishes for each other in the future, like what we may encounter in the next five years, and how we see our roles in each other's lives growing and changing on the road ahead. And so, we decided to write each other an open letter, without consulting each other or cheating, or even peeking.

We spoke from the heart and we told the truth. We hope our words will strike a chord with you or someone you love, beyond words.

Dear Francesca,

I love to look backwards, to the times when you were little, but it's even more fun to look forward. Because I think Frank Sinatra was right when he said the best is yet to come, and I'll tell you why.

But first, let me back up.

I know that I'm supposed to say that in the next five years, I look forward to you meeting a great guy, falling in love, and getting married, as well as continued success with your own writing, contributing stories to these memoirs, and finishing your own wonderful novel. I do want those things for you, but that's not the whole picture. Those are only the milestones, events in a life, like ticks on a time line, or pages in a photo album. And as great as those things are, what I want for you is harder to define and to achieve:

It's to know your own power, and to step fully into it.

You're an amazing young girl, from the inside out, from your hugely generous heart all the way to your very skin. I won't enumerate your many qualities here, because I tell you them all the time, and that would defeat my point anyway.

Because what I want for you in the near future is to know those qualities yourself, inside you.

To understand and enjoy the many things you're good at, and to believe in them, and ultimately, in yourself. To trust in your own judgment, to have confidence in your instincts and skills. To realize that it's not bragging to know you're good at something, and say so.

I say this because in my own life, I think that was a mistake I made, and one that many women make, not necessarily you. It took me until I was fifty-five to have this epiphany, and I'd like to save you twenty-five years.

And it matters now, more than ever. Because in the short run you'll have to make so many of those milestone decisions, like whom to marry.

I'm trying to save you from whom-to-divorce.

And how can I help you accomplish this? Where do I fit in? I suspect the answer is to get out of your way a little. I'm such an opinionated mom, from what to cook for dinner all the way to whom to vote for, and I need to shut up.

You don't need me to carry your raincoat to the movies anymore.

In fact, you don't need me to mother you anymore.

You're an adult, and you don't need me to raise you.

You need me to support you, as you raise yourself.

And so, in this curious and ironic way, I will do more, and less, as we go forward on our little journey together.

You're driving now.

And I'll pack the car with the things we need as we shuttle back and forth for visits; the summer clothes I'm storing at my house, plus the dogs, and maybe a fresh basil plant, because who doesn't need fresh basil?

But I won't bring art that isn't your taste, like I did last trip. Or clothing that is warm enough to wear in the Arctic, as is my wont.

And every mother's wont.

I'll be the best passenger ever.

Because you're the best driver ever.

Love, Mom

Dear Mom,

At twenty-five, I can't claim to have much worldly wisdom to impart to you, that's more your department. But there's never been I time I didn't know you, so it's safe to say I know you pretty well. And when I think about what's in store for you over the next five years, I see success, love, and motherhood, but I think you'll redefine all three. Here's what I see for you, what I wish for you, and what I want to be for you.

One of the things I admire most about you is how even after achieving success, you have all the energy and ambition of, well, a twenty-five-year-old. So I bet you'll reach an even higher career peak over the next five years. But I worry that you'll put more pressure on yourself in turn. Go easy. You had to do a balancing act when I was a kid, but now that you no longer have a teenager making demands or a college student whose school breaks dot your calendar, you can take advantage of this breathing room, even if it means keeping it as just that. By all means, chase what inspires you, write what moves you, but remember that there are many valid pursuits, some yet to be discovered. Be open to new passions and new loves.

Speaking of love, I hope and believe you will find romance in the next five years. You haven't put yourself out there much in terms of dating, but you can change that whenever you want to. You may make yourself more available, or I wouldn't be surprised if your charm attracts someone against your will; either way I think it will happen. At my stage in life, I'm putting myself out there constantly, and if you forget what that's like, let me remind you—you will have many horrible, boring, obnoxious dates. Do not be discouraged. It's part of the process and material for the books. And I know that if you get out there again, white knuckle it through a few weirdos and snoozefests, you will have a totally fantastic, magical date. It's a statistical certainty. But you have to play to win.

When you do find a man who holds your interest, listen to the advice you give me: Don't settle. I'm not worried about your putting up with a total jerk, that's a rookie mistake. But you may find yourself in a relationship with a great guy who is still not great for you, a guy who's close-but-no-cigar. Let that one go. Because age doesn't make a case for settling, it argues the opposite. You didn't go through the rise and fall of Thing One and Thing Two just to marry Thing Three. You're stronger than ever, wiser than before, and now you know what you want and need in a relationship—so ask for it, expect it, believe in it. Let your past experience guide you to the love you deserve and nothing less. Because you are smart, funny, and beautiful, and you deserve it all.

As for us? I see our relationship growing and deepening, while the essential bond remains the same. You're my mother, my hero, and my best friend, and I'll always want your input and advice. But whereas I used to look to you for the little stuff—a ride to play practice, blow-drying the back of my hair, making plane reservations—in the next five years, I'll look to you for life's more important questions, like, "Is this career shift the right move?" or "Do you think he'd make a good father?" I'm sure we'll still have stupid tiffs over silly things, but as I get older, I gain perspective, and that makes me value our closeness even more.

Maybe the main thing about our relationship that will change is the direction. When you were raising me, you had to tell me, teach me, guide me. Now that I'm an adult, let me be the one to reach to you. And you can trust that I always will.

But there I go again, thinking of how you'll help me, instead of how I can help you. I'm still getting the hang of this new direction myself. Although it can feel like there's greater distance between us, in reality I can offer you so much more now than I could when I was a kid, and I want to. As a child, I was a constant presence of walking, talking, needy love. Of course I still love you, but now I can offer you real friendship, even better than we've known before. I want to give you all the support you've always given me, guidance where I can, fun and joy everywhere else. Just don't ask for grandchildren. You've got at least ten years on that.

Love, Francesca

Acknowledgments

. . . .

We would like to express our love and gratitude to everyone at Macmillan and St. Martin's Press for supporting this book and its predecessors. First and foremost, thanks to Coach Jen Enderlin, our terrific editor, as well as to the brilliant John Sargent, Sally Richardson, Matthew Shear, Matt Baldacci, Brian Keller, Jeff Capshew, Michael Storrings, John Murphy, John Karle, and Sara Goodman. We appreciate so much your enthusiasm for these books, and we thank you for everything you do to support us.

We'd also like to thank Mary Beth Roche, Laura Wilson, Esther Bochner, Brant Janeway, and St. Martin's audiobook division, especially for giving us the opportunity to record our own audiobook, which is the way it should be done. An authentic voice will always ring true, and stories are meant to be told, not read, which is why we love audiobooks.

Huge thanks and love to our amazing agents, Molly Friedrich, Lucy Carson, and Molly Schulman of the Friedrich Agency. They're the smartest, funniest, and most loyal bunch you'll ever meet. God bless them for their great good hearts.

Thanks to *The Philadelphia Inquirer*, which carries our "Chick Wit" column, and to our editor, the wonderful Sandy Clark.

One of the biggest hearts in creation belongs to Laura Leonard, and her help, friendship, and love sustain us. Laura, thank you so much for all of your great comments and suggestions to this manuscript. We owe you, forever.

Love to our girlfriends, among them Nan Daley and Nora and Jolie Demchur, Paula Menghetti and Bev, Tori, and Alex, Franca Palumbo and Jessica Limbacher, and of course, Molly Friedrich and Julia, Lucy, and Pi-quy Carson. And thanks and love to Francesca's kitchen cabinet, Katy Andersen, Rebecca Harrington, and Courtney Yip (and the two men she trusts as brothers, Ryder Kessler and Marshall Roy), who help her navigate New York City and everything else. We're blessed in all of you.

Family is the heart of this book, because family is the heart of everything. Special thanks and love to Mother Mary and Brother Frank, and we still miss the late Frank Scottoline, though he is with us always.

Finally, thank you to our readers. We value your support so much, as well as all the stories of your own you've shared with us over the years. If you feel like you know us, you're right. In fact, you're one of the Flying Scottolines now, and we're stuck with each other.

We're family.

MEET ME AT EMOTIONAL BAGGAGE CLAIM

by Lisa Scottoline and Francesca Serritella

Behind the Novel

- "Mother Mary Knows Best":
  An Original Essay by Lisa Scottoline

Keep on Reading

- Ideas for Book Groups
- Reading Group Questions

For more reading group suggestions,
visit www.readinggroupgold.com.

 ST. MARTIN'S GRIFFIN

An Original Essay by the Author

"Mother Knows Best"
by Lisa Scottoline

If you have read this collection, you know that Mother Mary gives me lots of advice, some of it more useful than others. For example, Don't Put Too Much Food On Your Fork is not that helpful, since I lost my baby teeth. Watch Your Purse isn't always helpful either, especially since she often tells me this when no one is anywhere near us, in the produce aisle. But by far, the most useful advice she has ever given me is: Be Yourself. It's a profound little gem of wisdom, because it has so many applications—not only in everyday life but with respect to this book and writing in general.

If you ask me, and let's pretend you have, the most important thing in any writing is an original and authentic voice. If you are following Mother Mary's dictum and Being Yourself, you will write in an original and authentic voice. That voice comes from within, from your truest self, from your heart and soul. That's why good writers sound so different, one from the next. Modesty aside, I include Daughter Francesca and myself in that category, and you can see what I mean about voice by reading one of my contributions and one of hers, in this very collection. Though there are similarities between our voices, they are distinct. In fact, regardless of subject matter, you can tell whether Francesca or I wrote a particular story. Test yourself by covering the author with the top of your hand. I bet you got an A on the test.

Now, for people who are interested in writing or in understanding and appreciating books more deeply, the really interesting thing about voice is that voice transcends genre, subject matter, and every other classification. Those things are really superficial; those are the form atop the substance. That's why an author's voice can remain consistent regardless of whether the book is fiction, nonfiction, or just a story told over the telephone.

"Voice comes from within, from your truest self, from your heart and soul."

I didn't know this myself because I started my writing life as a novelist. I have been doing that for twenty-five years, writing a series of mystery novels about the women in a law firm called Rosato & Associates, as well as a series of emotional stories about family life that are not a series, which are called "stand-alones" in publishing. One genius critic compared both types of books, saying that the Rosato & Associates books are crime stories with a family subplot, and the emotional thrillers are family stories with a crime subplot.

Rewind for a moment, to a few years back, before I began to write these true-life stories with Francesca, like *Meet Me at Emotional Baggage Claim* and *Have A Nice Guilt Trip* (you can find an excerpt in the back of this book). Frankly, I wasn't sure I could make the transition from writing fiction to writing nonfiction. But then I heard a wonderful quote by the director Francis Ford Coppola, which I will paraphrase as "nothing in my movies ever happened, but all of it is true."

I realized that that's how I felt about my novels.

They weren't false at all. They were emotionally true, and each one sprang from something that took place in my life that caused me to feel some deep emotion, one powerful enough to drive a 90,000 word, full-length novel. Why am I telling you this?

I'll give you an honest answer, because you deserve nothing less, and if you have read me in these pages, you know I'm a fan of the truth. And the truth is that I hope you will give my novels a try. If you liked this collection, I know you will like my novels, and the reason I know that is because my voice is the same. The voice in these books is exactly the voice—or the heart and soul—as in the novels. And this is true whether the novel is a crime story with a family subplot, or a family story with a crime subplot. It doesn't matter. That's only the form atop the substance. The substance is voice—the connection between author's soul and a reader's soul—an invisible bond as strong as the cable on a suspension bridge.

So, if you would, please allow me to introduce you to my two latest novels. (You can find excerpts online; links listed below). One of them is *Accused*, the first novel in the Rosato & Associates series, which are the crime stories with the family subplot. In the book, lawyer Mary DiNunzio takes on the case of a young girl who believes that the man in prison for the murder of her older sister is, in fact, innocent. And at the same time, Mary has to decide if she really meant *yes* when she told her boyfriend she'd marry him. See what I mean about the family subplot? Love is involved, also three adorable octogenarians all named Tony called The Three Tonys. You'll meet them in the excerpt, and I have crushes on all of them, which is scary.

The other is my stand-alone novel *Keep Quiet*, a family story with this crime subplot, and it's an emotional thriller that follows what happens when a father who wants to be the Cool Dad says *yes* to his teenager when he shouldn't—and almost brings about the ruin of his family. That's the family story, but I won't give away the crime subplot here. You'll know exactly what I'm talking about if you read the excerpt.

Thank you very much for reading Francesca and me, and for sharing your hearts and souls with us. We appreciate each and every one of you, because you are more precious than you know. Thanks, too, for listening to my advice on writing and voice, and I hope those of you who wish to will write your own stories, whether they are literally true or not. We need more voices in this world, each of us telling a story from the heart, so don't ever second-guess yourself, should you decide to write one down. Go for it, and always remember what Mother Mary said.

Not about watching your purse.

Be yourself.

> "We need more voices in this world, each of us telling a story from the heart."

Accused
http://us.macmillan.com/accusedarosatoassociatesnovel
LisaScottoline

Keep Quiet
http://us.macmillan.com/keepquiet/LisaScottoline

Now Available, in hardcover, from St. Martin's Press

Ideas for Book Groups

I am a huge fan of book clubs because it means
people are reading and discussing books. Mix that
with wine and carbs, and you can't keep me away.
I'm deeply grateful to all who read me, and especially honored when my book is chosen by a book club.
I wanted an opportunity to say thank you to those
who read me, which gave me the idea of a contest.
Every year I hold a book club contest and the winning book club gets a visit from me and a night of
fabulous food and good wine. To enter is easy: all
you have to do is take a picture of your entire book
club with each member holding a copy of my newest
hardcover and send it to me by mail or e-mail. No
book club is too small or too big. Don't belong to a
book club? Start one. Just grab a loved one, a neighbor or friend, and send in your picture of you each
holding my newest book. I look forward to coming
to your town and wining and dining your group.
For more details, just go to www.scottoline.com.

Tour time is my favorite time of year because I get to
break out my fancy clothes and meet with interesting
and fun readers around the country. The rest of the
year I am a homebody, writing every day, but thrilled
to be able to connect with readers through e-mail.
I read all my e-mail, and answer as much as I can.
So, drop me a line about books, families, pets, love,
or whatever is on your mind at lisa@scottoline.com.
For my latest book and tour information, special
promotions, and updates you can sign up at www.
scottoline.com for my newsletter.

Jisa Scottoline

The Bunnies Book Club of Scottsdale, AZ,
submit their photo for Lisa's book club contest.

 *Reading Group Questions*

Reading
Group
Gold

1. Lisa writes, in her title essay, that "precious few books are devoted to a mother's relationship with her adult child," a fact that she finds "crazy" since the mother-daughter bond becomes "more important, not less, as time goes on." But Lisa acknowledges that we bring our own emotional baggage into our relationships. Lisa's is her need to nag. What is *your* relationship like with your own mothers, or daughters (or sons)? What emotional baggage do you think you have brought into your relationships, and how do you think it effects your relationships?

2. In the essay "Shakespeare Was No Dummy," Lisa discovers that Mother Mary's official name was different than she thought. Have you had any experiences similar to Lisa's, in which you find out something really surprising about your parent later in life? Lisa goes on to discuss how important names are, and how they can impact our identity, and/or our children's identities. What are your favorite names, and why? If you could change your name to any name you want, what would it be? Did you, or do you, have baby names chosen for your child before you ever had any? What are they, and what do you like about them?

3. In "I Love You, Man," Francesca jokes about the "manly" side of her friendship with Lisa. How do men and women's friendships differ? What stereotypes are designated to men and women in regard to their friendships and how true do you think they are? What special things do you do with your friends that define the uniqueness of your relationship?

*Keep on
Reading*

4. In Lisa's essay, "Happy Birthday," she reflects on getting older, and admires the strength she sees in her aging and more fragile mother. What lessons can we learn from our parents' generation? In what ways do you see yourself in your parent(s)? Which attributes of theirs would you like to emulate, and in what ways would you like to be different?

5. Francesca writes about the ups and downs of living in a big city and about the challenges of connecting in such a large and anonymous place. What advice would you give to Francesca in regard to city living? How would your advice differ if she were living in a suburb? Where do you think young people should go to meet people? What are the benefits of living in new and different places? What are the challenges? Tell about your experiences.

6. Lisa and Francesca both write about their summer with Mother Mary. There are some laugh-out-loud moments, some very cranky exchanges, and some tender times, but every minute, even the arguments, are fueled by love. What are your favorite memories with your parents, and which ones do you treasure the most? Which one would you go back and change if you could?

7. Often there are historic events that become defining moments in our collective consciousness, and Francesca writes a very moving and insightful essay about 9/11. Which major historic event had the most impact on you? Where were you when you learned the news? How did the event change you?

 *Reading Group Questions*

Reading
Group
Gold

8. Throughout the book, Lisa and Francesca share stories about their family including Mother Mary and Brother Frank. But, in "Bittersweet," Lisa talks about having two families, the one you are born into, and the one you create. Who in your life do you consider family? How do those relationships differ from those with your actual family members?

9. In "Skype Appeal," Francesca gives us a look at what it's like to date in today's modern technological world. In what ways do you think dating is easier, and in what ways is it harder? Has technology improved communications between couples, or made it more difficult? How?

Keep on Reading

10. Lisa and Francesca write deeply felt and moving letters to each other at the conclusion of this book. They set forth what they wish for each other in the future, and the letters are saturated with love and concern. If you were writing a similar letter, to whom would you write it, and what would you say? Who do you think would write a letter to you, and what would they say to you?

Turn the page for a sneak peek at the next novel by
Lisa Scottoline and Francesca Serritella

Available Summer 2014

Foreword

· · · · · · · · · · · · · · · ·

By Lisa

Nobody knows more about guilt than women.

Especially, this woman.

I don't have the time or space to list all of the things I feel guilty about, and I even feel guilty about that.

So I'll narrow it down and name only the things that I feel guilty about since dinner:

I feel guilty that I ate second helpings of rigatoni.

I feel guilty that I used tomato sauce from a jar.

I feel guilty that I didn't wash out the jar completely before I put it in recycling.

I feel guilty that I ran the dishwasher when it wasn't completely full.

Also, did I mention that Daughter Francesca is home visiting, and I feel especially guilty that I served my only child such a crappy dinner?

There is no guilt like Mom Guilt.

We are always failing our children in some way, aren't we?

At least I am.

Start with the fact that my daughter is an Only Child. I didn't give her any siblings, and that was because I divorced her father, whom I call Thing One.

Divorce Guilt.

I even divorced her stepfather, Thing Two.

Double Divorce Guilt!

(But don't worry, I bought her a lot of stuff to make up for it.)

Bottom line, if you're a mom, you'll feel guilty all the time, and this is true because you're a daughter as well, and God only knows how many times you failed your poor mother.

Shame on you, and guilt, too.

Now, to come to my point. If you think I'm going to preach to you that guilt is a bad thing, you're wrong.

I don't want you to change.

Because I like you just the way you are.

Don't lose your guilt. Embrace it, like me.

I don't feel guilty for feeling guilty.

I've long ago accepted that guilt is a part of me, like cellulite.

Guilt makes me work harder, do more errands, and get to the dry cleaner's before closing.

Guilt means I'm always early, everywhere.

Guilt makes me pay my bills on time.

Guilt makes me nicer to people.

Guilt helps me be a better mother.

Guilt gets me on the elliptical. Occasionally, but only on Level One.

Guilt makes the journey of life into one long guilt trip. But in a nice way.

Hence the title of this book, *Have a Nice Guilt Trip*.

Herein you'll find true and funny stories from Daughter Francesca and me about life, both together and apart, since at twenty-seven years old, she has not only moved out, but stopped nursing.

We'll also tell a few silly and/or poignant tales about my

mother, Mother Mary, who travels with a back scratcher and an attitude.

My guess is that our family will remind you of your family, except we're less well-behaved.

So read on, and join us for the trip.

And come as you are.

Homely Remedies

· · · · · · · · · · · · · · · · ·

By Lisa

I hate it when Mother Mary is right, which is always.

We begin a zillion years ago, when I'm a little kid with a bad cold, and Mother Mary goes instantly for the Vicks VapoRub. As a child, I had more Vicks Vapo rubbed on me than most consumptives. My chest was as shiny as a stripper's and even more fragrant.

Camphor is still my favorite perfume.

Which could be why I'm single.

Another favorite home remedy of hers was the do-it-yourself humidifier. By this I mean she placed a Pyrex baking dish full of water on every radiator in the house.

I never knew why, and neither did my friends. None of them had radiators, because they had nicer houses. They had something called forced air, which sounded vaguely scary to us. The Flying Scottolines never forced anything, especially something you needed to breathe.

And in the summer, those same people had central air, which was something else we didn't have. Our air lacked centralization. The only central thing in our house was Mother Mary, and that was how she liked it.

But back to the do-it-yourself humidifiers, which sat like an open-air fishbowl on every radiator. As a child, I understood that this would cure something dreadful called Dry Air, which we had in spades. I didn't really understand why Uncle Mikey had to move to Arizona for the Dry Air, when he could've just moved to our house, but be that as it may, I was grateful that I had an all-knowing mother, who understood that air came in forced, central, and dry, and that everything could be cured by Pyrex.

The only time this was a problem was on Sundays, when Mother Mary actually wanted to bake ziti or eggplant parm, and there were no dishes available except for the ones cooking water on the radiators. She would dispatch me to get a Pyrex dish off the radiator and wash it out, and I would do so happily, if the end result was eggplant parm.

I will still do anything for eggplant parm.

Make a note, should we meet.

But back to the story, cleaning the baking dishes was a yucky job. Often the water in the dishes would have dried up, leaving a scummy residue, and even if there was some water left, it wasn't a pretty sight. Dog and cat hair would be floating on the surface, or ash from a passing cigarette.

According to Mother Mary, smoking was fine for air quality.

You win some, you lose some.

So fast forward to when I become a mother myself, and baby Francesca gets sick, and of course Mother Mary advocates Vicks and Pyrex, but I reject these ideas as old-fashioned. I am Modern.

Enter antibiotics.

I had that kid so pumped up with amoxicillin she could've grown mold. In fact, I had her on them prophylactically, so she'd never get another ear infection, and if I could have her on them now, I would, so she'd never get pregnant.

I'm kidding.

It's a joke, okay?

But then recently, I got the worst cold ever, and I called the doctor, who told me that antibiotics weren't such a hot idea and what I really needed was Vicks VapoRub and a humidifier. I couldn't believe my ears. I wanted the magic pill to make it all better but he says that it's a virus and all that, and no.

I didn't tell this to Mother Mary. Don't you, either.

I supposed I could just get a Pyrex dish and put it on the radiator, but I am still Modern and I refuse. Also the doctor says I need a cool mist humidifier, and not a warm mist humidifier, and once again, I feel lucky to learn more about the mysteries of air, which now comes in mist.

Who knew oxygen could be so complicated?

So I go to the drug store, buy the requisite cool mist humidifier, and bring it home. I spend exactly one night with this thing and want to shoot myself. It's thirty degrees outside, and in my bedroom, it's twenty. An Arctic chill blasts from the cool mist humidifier, and I'm up all night.

So I go back to the drugstore and buy a warm mist humidifier. I take it home, and it frizzes my hair, but you can't have everything. Also, it comes with a little slot for a stick that's impregnated with Vicks VapoRub, and you know what I'm thinking.

This is the revenge of Mother Mary.

> "The tell-all twosome have yet again opened their hearts and homes, cooking up a huge helping of laughs, sprinkled with a few tears and a dash of motherly love—and it all goes down deliciously."
> —*Booklist*

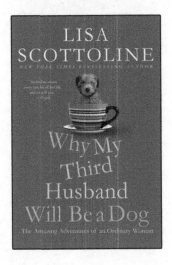

St. Martin's Press   St. Martin's Griffin

No one does
EMOTIONAL, POWERFUL, HEARTBREAKING,
or HONEST like *New York Times* bestselling author

LISA SCOTTOLINE

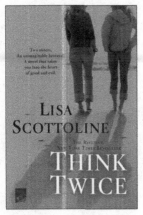

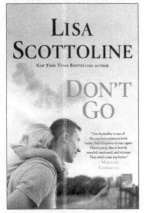

COMING IN HARDCOVER